BRITAIN'S
DAY-FLYIN

A field guide to the
of Britain and

David Newland, Robert Still & Andy Swash

Technical Adviser: Mark Parsons (Butterfly Conservation)
Principal photographers: Paul Brock, David Green,
David Newland, Mark Parsons, Keith Tailby

WILDGuides

PRINCETON
press.princeton.edu

Published by Princeton University Press,
41 William Street, Princeton, New Jersey 08540
In the United Kingdom: Princeton University Press, 6 Oxford Street,
Woodstock, Oxfordshire OX20 1TW
nathist.press.princeton.edu

British Library Cataloging-in-Publication Data is available

Library of Congress Control Number 2012956137
ISBN 978-0-691-15832-7

Production and design by **WILD**Guides Ltd., Old Basing, Hampshire UK.
Printed in China

10 9 8 7 6 5 4 3 2 1

Contents

A Hummingbird Hawk-moth in flight

Preface

At the Great Exhibition of 1851, Queen Victoria was captivated by an exhibition of the world's hummingbirds. None of these exquisite little birds lives anywhere near Britain and Ireland but there is a moth that looks just like one – it is called the Hummingbird Hawk-moth. This little 'hummer', so similar to a hummingbird, hovers in front of a flower, its long tongue reaching out to drink nectar. Its golden wings whirr so fast that they are almost invisible. Suddenly it disappears, lost to sight, only to return again, just as suddenly, to the next flower. On a sunny day in summer they may pop up almost anywhere in Britain and Ireland, occasionally even in gardens. So there is every chance that you will see one of these exciting moths.

Britain and Ireland has more than twice as many species of day-flying 'larger' moths than butterflies, and considerably more if the tiny 'micro-moths' are taken into consideration. They are fantastically varied in colour, size and habits and some of the species put their butterfly relatives very much in the shade when it comes to colourful finery.

There are already many good books about moths to choose from, but, to our knowledge, this is the first book that specifically concentrates on day-flying moths. In producing it, we have endeavoured to provide accurate and concise information, and to present this in an accessible form for anyone interested in nature who would like to find out more about these fabulous creatures and see them flying in the wild.

Many people have contributed to the production of this book and are included with our grateful thanks in a detailed list of acknowledgements at the end of the book. But we would particularly like to highlight here our debt to Butterfly Conservation, which is the leading European organization involved in conservation and research on butterflies and moths. Details about the work of Butterfly Conservation are included in a section towards the back of the book.

Butterfly Conservation's Head of Moth Conservation, Mark Parsons, has reviewed the text and helped us greatly by his comments and suggestions. Many photographers have also generously made available their images. These are an essential part of the book and without these wonderful photos, it could not have been completed. The names of the main contributing photographers are listed on the title page, and there is a list of credits for each individual photograph at the back of the book.

Our thanks go to everyone who has contributed, but responsibility for the design of the book and the accuracy of the information it contains rests entirely with ourselves.

We hope that this book will provide a useful introduction to the extraordinary beauty and diversity of moths, and particularly those that can be seen during the day.

David Newland
Ickleton
Cambridgeshire

Robert Still
Old Basing
Hampshire

Andy Swash
West Hill
Devon

March 2013

The difference between butterflies and moths

CLOCKWISE FROM TOP LEFT:

Brimstone butterfly resting with its wings together; its antennae have curved and thickened ends.

Lesser Treble Bar moth resting with its wings flat, pressed against a branch and its antennae folded back.

Oak Eggar moth in resting pose with its wings and antennae folded down.

Holly Blue butterfly with wings together above its body and showing its clubbed antennae.

Butterflies and moths are both members of the scientific order Lepidoptera and have many similarities. The few differences are outlined below but it is important to note that it is usually possible to find exceptions to every 'rule'. Indeed, in France moths are called *papillons de la nuit*, which translates as "butterflies of the night"!

Butterflies almost always only fly during the day. Most moths fly at night and only a minority of species habitually fly during the day (or are readily disturbed from rest and then fly, perhaps for some time, before settling again).

Most butterflies have club-shaped antennae – a straight rod with a knob on the end. By comparison, each antenna of a moth is a filament, sometimes curved, without a knob. In many species the male's antennae are feathery, an adaptation that enhances their ability to detect the scent of females.

Most butterflies rest with their wings held together above their bodies. Moths usually fold their wings down alongside their bodies.

Another difference between butterflies and moths is their wing structures. In butterflies the four wings are completely separate, whereas in most moths, the pair of wings on each side of the body are connected very near the body by a small 'hook'. This 'hook' is a short bristle on the front edge of the hindwing that engages with a 'catch' attached to the forewing. This feature is usually impossible to see with the naked eye but causes both wings to beat together when the moth flies.

The coupling between the forewing and hindwing of a typical moth (image shows the underside of the wings of a male **Large Yellow Underwing** *Noctua pronuba*: female moths have a slightly different coupling).

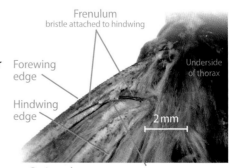

Frenulum
bristle attached to hindwing

Forewing edge

Hindwing edge

Underside of thorax

2 mm

Retinaculum catch formed by strap on forewing

What is a day-flying moth?

About 2,500 moth species have been recorded in Britain and Ireland, including 1,600 so-called 'micro-moths'. However, since the majority of species fly at night most people are only likely to come across a small number of them. Those that are most likely to be encountered are the species that fly during the day, and it is these moths that are the subject of this book.

But what constitutes a 'day-flying' moth is often open to question. In many cases there is no doubt that a moth is a day-flyer – foresters and burnets, for example, are on the wing whenever it is sunny, just like butterflies. However, many species that do not usually fly in daylight will regularly do so during the day if they are disturbed, sometimes for quite long periods. Such disturbance can be quite accidental, while walking over heathland or brushing against branches, and sometimes large numbers of the same species may be seen. This makes it difficult to compile a definitive list of day-flying moths.

Although there is no absolute dividing line, 133 species of 'macro-moths' are generally regarded as day-flyers. These are all included in this book. Many 'micro-moths' are also day-flyers but, as their name suggests, they tend to be very small and are also often very difficult to identify (see *page 176* for an explanation of the difference between macro- and micro-moths). For this reason, only 22 species of day-flying micro-moths are included in the book. These are the species that are most likely to be encountered or which illustrate the tremendous diversity of this

ABOVE: The **Jersey Tiger** has been spreading in southern England and is now found in London. It often frequents gardens and allotments, where its brightly coloured wings are easy to see.

BELOW: The **Vapourer** is a common moth. Males may appear almost anywhere late in the season, but females cannot fly and stay close to their old cocoon.

complex group. For example, although there are many different species of grass-moth that are readily disturbed during the day, just one, the Hook-streak Grass-veneer has been covered in detail. Other grass-moths look very similar and may be impossible to distinguish without a good photograph or without netting a specimen for examination.

Towards the end of the book is a list of other reference books and useful websites that will be helpful in identifying the species that are not included here, or provide additional information that will help to confirm an identification (see *pages 215–217*).

Many day-flying moths are widespread and fairly common, and only a few are really rare – but it still helps to know when and where to look. You may want to try and find all the 155 species in this book – good luck if this is your aim. But for many people, just being able to identify the moths they see when out and about, whether in town or country, in a garden or a meadow or a wood, will bring rewards. The aim of this book is to help everyone in their quest, whatever their level of interest.

Moth biology

Like all insects, moths and butterflies do not have a backbone. Instead, they have a hard outer casing that is called the exoskeleton. Their bodies have three parts: head (at the front), thorax (in the middle) and abdomen (at the rear). The head has the insect's eyes, its proboscis (tongue) for drinking nectar (if it has one, not all species do) and its two antennae. The antennae are sensory organs that, amongst other functions, can detect smell. In males, the antennae have a particular role in sensing the presence of a female by detecting her scent (pheromones).

The digestive tract and reproductive organs of a moth are in the abdomen, which is the largest of the three body parts. Small openings (spiracles) in the sides of the thorax and abdomen allow the insect to breathe.

All moths have four wings, two on each side of their body (although the females of some species have just vestigial wings and, as a consequence, are flightless). The wings are attached to the thorax, which contains powerful muscles to drive them. The moth's six legs are also attached to the thorax.

Moths (and butterflies) are cold-blooded creatures. Their body temperature is close to the prevailing ambient temperature. However they are able to vibrate their wing muscles in order to warm up. By doing this, they can raise their local thorax temperature several degrees above ambient, perhaps by as much as 10°C. This is enough to allow them to fly on cold days.

Silver Y moth nectaring on lavender, with its principal body parts labelled

The life-cycle of a moth

A moth's reproductive cycle is the same as it is for a butterfly. Females lay eggs on or near their caterpillars' foodplant. Caterpillars hatch from the eggs, usually after a few weeks. They eat steadily, often for some months, shedding their skin several times as they gradually grow bigger until, when fully grown, they pupate (that is, turn into a pupa). Sometimes they have first spun a silken cocoon around themselves for protection. They remain as a pupa while the process of metamorphosis runs its course and the dormant caterpillar turns into an adult moth – a process that can take weeks or even months. Then the pupal casing splits open and the moth emerges. For another hour or two, each newly emerged moth has to wait while its crumpled wings unfold and harden into their final shape. Then it can fly, males to look for females and females to look for a suitable habitat in which to lay their eggs. Male moths usually emerge before females, and so are ready to mate and fertilize the females' eggs at the earliest opportunity. And so the whole reproductive cycle begins again.

This cycle usually lasts for a year (although occasionally for two years, or sometimes for just a few months in species that have more than one brood each year). Depending on the species, it overwinters either as an egg, caterpillar, pupa or adult moth. The flight season for adult moths varies from species to species. Some fly for long periods, from spring to autumn (perhaps having more than one brood), whereas others are on the wing for only a few weeks at a particular time of year. Information on flight seasons is given in the species accounts.

Six-spot Burnet life-cycle

Eggs

Adults mating

Newly hatched caterpillars (larvae)

Newly emerged adult beside its pupal case and cocoon

Caterpillar (larva)

Pupa

9

The naming of moths

Biologists have a systematic way of classifying all living things. The method they use stems from the idea of a hierarchical tree. One branch of the tree is for all the insects in the world – and there are an enormous number of them. In fact, over a million different species of insects have been recorded (although, astonishingly, researchers suggest that there may be twice as many more waiting to be discovered*).

The insect branch of the hierarchical tree has numerous lower branches. Each lower branch represents a different group of insects. The group that includes all the butterflies and moths is the branch labelled *Lepidoptera*, a name derived from old Greek words meaning 'scaled wings'. This feature alone distinguishes butterflies and moths from all other groups of insects.

The branch (or *Order*) *Lepidoptera* divides further into many more branches. These are called *Super-families*. Each *Super-family* branch is further divided into many *Family* branches, which in turn divide into *Genus* branches and finally into a branch for each *species*. Sometimes there may be an intermediate branch between the *Family* and the *Genus* called a *Sub-family* branch, which collects together a group of similar genera (the plural of genus).

Scaly wings

When you look closely at a moth's wings with the naked eye, you can't usually see any scales – just a fine pattern. But under higher magnification, both sides of the membrane of every wing are found to be covered with very tiny coloured flakes. They are all arranged neatly in rows and look like a miniature roof with lots of separate tiles. These tiny scales are formed only a day or two before each new adult moth emerges from its pupa. What's more, the white and blue scales (if there are any) form first, then the yellow and red scales, and lastly the very dark and black scales. This has been discovered in the laboratory by carefully observing the changes that take place in the last few days before an adult insect emerges from its dormant pupa.

Wing scales of a Garden Tiger moth *Arctia caja* at 55× magnification

So, all our moth species are grouped into genera and families, sometimes with sub-families in between. For example, there are 7 different species of burnet moth in Britain and Ireland. They are all coloured red and black, are similar in shape and have the same curved antennae. They may well have arisen by evolution over many millennia from just one species. They are all in the genus *Zygaena*. This genus is in the sub-family called *Zygaeninae*. That sub-family is part of the larger family *Zygaenidae* which, worldwide, contains about 800 different species and includes the forester moths, which are all green and are grouped within the sub-family *Procidinae*.

In the species accounts that follow, the most widely used English names are given, with the species' scientific name that comprises two parts: the genus and species names.

*Source: Stuart Reynolds, *60 years of Insects: Entomology in the new Elizabethan Era*, Presidential Address, Royal Entomological Society, 2012

For example, the scientific name of the Six-spot Burnet is *Zygaena filipendulae*.

Populations of some species can become geographically separated and, as a consequence, are no longer able to interbreed. Over many years, small differences may occur in appearance, preferred habitat or breeding cycle, and taxonomists distinguish between these different populations by giving them *subspecies* names. Quite often, moths (and butterflies) that occur in Britain and Ireland are a subspecies of a species that is found elsewhere in the world. For example, the British population of the Six-spot Burnet has been given the subspecies name *stephensi* and so its scientific name is extended to *Zygaena filipendulae* ssp. *stephensi*.

Sometimes different forms of the same species exist together in the same place. The Latticed Heath *Chiasmia clathrata* is a good example. As well as its customary form with obviously chequered upperwings, the moth occasionally has darker brown wings and looks quite different, with its chequered pattern suppressed. This is due to a genetic variation. The unusual version is said to be a different *form* of the same species and is given an additional name, hence *Chiasmia clathrata* f. *alboguttata*.

The simple test of whether two moths belong to different species is whether, if populations of each are brought together, they do not interbreed and produce viable offspring. However, like most things in nature, this is not an infallible test.

Taxonomic classifications are constantly changing as new information becomes available, and you may find that the name of a moth used in this book is not the same as that used in other publications.

Taxonomy

Scientists responsible for classifying living things are called taxonomists, and what they do is to study taxonomy. The founding father of taxonomy was the Swedish botanist Carl Linnaeus (1707–1778) who proposed many of the hierarchical branches that we still use today. As new information comes to light, taxonomists may have to revise their conclusions. As a result, a particular species may be moved from one genus to another reflecting the discovery of new characteristics. The science of DNA fingerprinting has introduced a completely new dimension to taxonomy, and it is likely that there will be more changes in classification in the years ahead as new genetic data become available.

Scientific nomenclature

One of the consequences of having a formal scheme of classification is that it gives a framework for naming moths. Each different species has an English name, such as Six-spot Burnet. But that is not the scientific name, which, in full, includes the order, super-family, family, sub-family (if there is one) and genus names, as well as the species name. So Six-spot Burnet is: *Lepidoptera, Zygaenoidea, Zygaenidae, Zygaeninae, Zygaena filipendulae*. The order is *Lepidoptera*, the super-family name is *Zygaenoidea*, the family name is *Zygaenidae*, the sub-family is *Zygaeninae*, the genus is *Zygaena* and the species name is *filipendulae*. By long-standing convention, the genus and species names are written in italics, with the genus name starting with a capital letter and the species name all in lower-case. In formal scientific publications it is also customary to add, after the species name, the name of the person who first described the species and the date that its description was first published.

English names

The convention used throughout this book for English names (whether moth or plant names) is to show specific names with Initial Capitals and general names in lower case. This helps to avoid confusion when specific names as opposed to general terms are used (*e.g.* distinguishing between the Forester and forester moths in general).

Identifying moths

The day-flying moths in this book have been grouped by their general appearance and by family. A group may consist of only one family or of several families with similar characteristics. The group that includes the largest number of day-flying moths species is the geometrids (60 species), and that with the smallest number is the hawk-moths, only three of which fly during the day. The eight groups appear in this book in the order shown in this table.

1. **Foresters & Burnets**

2. **Clearwings**

3. **Eggars, Emperor, Kentish Glory & Hook-tips**

4. **Geometrids**

5. **Hawk-moths**

6. **Tussocks, Footmen, Tigers & Ermines**

7. **Noctuids**

8. **Micro-moths**

To identify moths, it is important to have an appreciation of how much they can vary in size. The largest of the day-flyers is the Oak Eggar, which has a forewing length (often abbreviated as FL) of 25–34 mm. As is the case for some other species, females are bigger than males and can be up to 25% larger. Next in size is the Emperor Moth, which is slightly smaller by a millimetre or two. Again, females are larger than males.

In contrast, micro-moths are generally very small. The smallest day-flyer in this book is the Horse-chestnut Leaf-miner. Although there may be many buzzing round a Horse-chestnut tree in mid-summer, they are easily missed as they are so tiny; their forewing length is just 4 mm.

The table on *pages 14–15* summarizes the main features that distinguish the different groups of day-flying moth and the families or sub-families within each group. Although the information is very much simplified, and there are many exceptions, it aims to provide a useful starting point for identification.

Within each family, there is usually a fair degree of uniformity, not only of size, but also of general appearance. However, identifying which family a moth belongs to will often be easier than deciding what species it is. For example, recognizing a moth as a forester or a burnet should be fairly straightforward, but distinguishing between the different forester and burnet species can be difficult. Similarly, there is no doubt about a moth being a clearwing, as this group mimics bees and wasps, but determining which species is often challenging. Two of the other groups, the geometrids and noctuids, often lead to identification difficulties, primarily because they contain so many species that look superficially similar.

Measuring size

The traditional measurement used for moths was 'wingspan'. This was derived from measuring the tip-to-tip forewing dimension of dead specimens pinned in a display cabinet. A more consistent and easier measurement is the forewing length of a live specimen, and that is the approach adopted in this book. Forewing length (sometimes abbreviated as FL) is measured from where the wing is attached to the thorax to the upper corner of its free edge (apex).

Of course, like people, moths of the same species differ in size, so the measurement given is an indication of the range in length rather than an absolute measure. In addition to giving the forewing length in millimetres, this dimension is also shown at full scale by a ruled line, which helps to give an immediate impression of the size of moth you are looking for.

To identify a moth it is important to consider all the evidence you can gather. Having established its size, look for how the moth positions its wings if it settles. Geometrids usually look flatter than noctuids, which fold their wings against their bodies; they also tend to have slim bodies, while those of noctuids are stouter. After size and shape, look for colour and pattern. In many cases, brown is the predominant colour. But look carefully at the pattern on the wings and, with practice, you will learn to distinguish what, initially, seem to be only small or insignificant differences. Then look for any behavioural clues and consider the habitat in which you have found a moth. When you have a provisional identification check whether the species is to be expected in that location, whether the right foodplant for its caterpillars is nearby, and whether the time of year is appropriate.

A complication is that, as moths age, they lose scales and their colours fade. Then it may be difficult or impossible to be certain about their identity. A good photograph may help for comparison with the images here or on apps and websites (see *page 217*). Modern compact cameras and smartphone cameras will usually capture entirely satisfactory images for this purpose.

Some moth enthusiasts carry a net to permit them to examine specimens close-up. If you wish to do this, be sure to check that the species is not legally protected (see the *Conservation and legislation* section on *page 210*) and that any necessary permissions from landowners have been obtained. If you do catch specimens for examination, do release them unharmed where you found them, away from the eyes of possible predators.

Identification checklist

Size	Shape	Colour
Pattern	Behaviour	Habitat
Location	Foodplant	Time of year

Typical geometrid resting position:
Yellow Shell

Typical noctuid resting position:
Silver Y

Macros and micros

The terms macro-moth and micro-moth are often used when referring to moths. This is not a taxonomic division, but rather an arbitrary distinction based on size, with families that contain mainly very small species being called micro-moths. (See *page 176* for further explanation.)

13

Day-flying moth groups – the key distinguishing features

Page	Family or Sub-family		No. of day-flying species	Distinguishing features	Forewing length
Group: Foresters & Burnets					
30	**Foresters** (*Procridinae*)		3	Narrow green wings held close to the body when at rest	About 12 mm; females slightly shorter than males
33	**Burnets** (*Zygaeninae*)		7	Narrow red-and-black wings held close to the body when at rest	About 16 mm; male and female the same size
Group: Clearwings					
40	**Clearwings** (*Sesiidae*)		16	Transparent wings held tightly against a thin body; look similar to a hoverfly or small wasp	10–20 mm depending on the species
Group: Eggars, Emperor, Kentish Glory & Hook-tips					
60	**Eggars** (*Lasiocampidae*)		2	Large, usually with golden-brown wings	Up to 40 mm in female Oak Eggar; males shorter
62	**Emperor** (*Saturniidae*)		1	A colourful species with a pronounced eye on each of its four wings (Emperor Moth)	Varies from 27 mm for a small male up to 41 mm for a large female
63	**Kentish Glory** (*Endromidae*)		1	Brown and white (Kentish Glory)	Slightly shorter than the Emperor Moth
64	**Hook-tips** (*Drepanidae*)		2	Golden-brown with a pronounced hook-shaped curve at the tip of the forewings	Around 16 mm; much shorter than other moths in this group
Group: Geometrids					
66	**Geometrids** (*Geometridae*)		60	A variable group with slender bodies and wings held flat	Usually in the range 15–20 mm

| 128 | **Hawk-moths** (*Sphingidae*) |  | 3 | Hovering flight and sudden movements; smaller than their nocturnal relatives | About 22 mm, male and female the same |

136	**Tussocks** (*Lymantriidae*)		3	Males are brown with heavily feathered antennae (female Vapourer are wingless)	15 mm (male Vapourer) up to 30 mm (Gypsy Moth)
139	**Footmen** (*Arctiidae Lithosiinae*)		2	Black wings with a red collar, the wings held tightly wrapped around a slender body (Red-necked Footman); orange/yellow with small black spots (Dew Moth)	16 mm
141	**Tigers** (*Arctiidae Arctiinae*)		5	Forewings are brown-and-white, striped like a tiger; rest with forewings covering the more colourful hindwings	30 mm the longest and 15 mm the shortest
146	**Ermines** (*Arctiidae Arctiinae*)		2	Generally smaller than tigers with wing colouring similar to ermine robes (Clouded Buff and Muslin Moth)	About 20 mm

| 148 | **Noctuids** (*Noctuidae*) | | 26 | Mainly brown, broad-bodied and medium-sized. At rest, the forewings are held close to the body and cover the hindwings, usually overlapping each other slightly | Typically about 20 mm |

| 176 | **Micro-moths** (includes many different families) |  | 22 | Very variable, but all small, some very small | 4–16 mm depending on species; usually obviously shorter than most macro-moths |

Where to look for day-flying moths

Although moths are generally less frequently seen during the day than butterflies, they are about if you know where to look. Some species are much more choosy about where they live than others, so a little knowledge of the types of habitat in which day-flying moths are found can be invaluable. These habitats can be divided into eight broad categories, each of which is illustrated in this section. The species accounts in this book includes a box headed *Where found* that gives a more precise indication of the habitat(s) that the species favours and therefore where it is most likely to be encountered.

1. Gardens and parkland: look anywhere in gardens, public open spaces, parkland and orchards, particularly where there is an abundance of flowers and a diversity of vegetation structure.

2. Meadows and farmland: explore areas of mixed farmland particularly where there are conservation areas with flowery grassland, especially in the shelter of hedgerows; it is also worth investigating dry and wet grassland, water meadows, waste ground, and road verges.

3. Downland: a number of day-flying moths favour chalk downland with short grass and open ground, downland scrub and old quarries; the term calcareous grassland includes limestone as well as chalk soils.

4. Heathland and moorland: the generally acidic soils and sometimes boggy conditions support rather impoverished plant communities compared with other soil types, but these habitats can be some of the best places to look for day-flying moths, including localized species.

5. Woodland: broad-leaved and coniferous woods with open, sunny clearings and rides are often excellent places to look for day-flying moths, particularly in the lowlands.

6. Coastal habitats: dunes, saltmarshes, steep slopes and cliffs, including rocky places, ravines and gorges, can harbour day-flying moths, including some rare and local species.

7. Wetland and fenland: some day-flying moths particularly favour reedbeds and areas of marshy ground or flood meadows, including adjacent wooded or scrubby areas.

8. Uplands: some day-flying moths live only in the hills and mountains of northern Britain; this habitat category includes high moorland, and upland bogs and woodland.

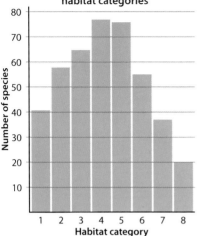

Number of species found in different habitat categories

Number of species (y-axis: 10, 20, 30, 40, 50, 60, 70, 80)

Habitat category (x-axis: 1, 2, 3, 4, 5, 6, 7, 8)

1. Gardens and parkland
2. Meadows and farmland
3. Downland
4. Heathland and moorland
5. Woodland
6. Coastal habitats
7. Wetland and fenland
8. Uplands

The chart *above* shows the number of different species of day-flying moth that may be found in the eight habitat categories illustrated on the previous pages. For the species covered in this book, most will be found on heathland and moorland (77 species), and almost as many (76 species) can be expected in woodland habitats. Some of these (47 species) are the same because many day-flying moths occur in both habitat types. At least 41 day-flying moths appear from time to time in gardens and parks. This is about twice as many as the number of butterfly species that are seen regularly in gardens. The habitat with the lowest number of different moth species is, not surprisingly, the upland mountains of northern England and Scotland. But there are some interesting and attractive montane species that can reward enthusiastic searching!

Each species account provides details of the *Larval foodplants*. But it does not always follow that if you find a foodplant in the preferred habitat you will find the moth you are searching for. What is true, though, is that if you are sure a foodplant is not present, the moth you are looking for is unlikely to be found.

Looking for clues

When interpreting the species accounts and what is said about *Where found* and *Larval foodplants*, it is important to consider all the information provided for that species.

For example, the summary boxes in the species account for the Four-spotted moth are as follows:

Where found: Warm, dry, open ground with sparse vegetation and broken soil
Larval foodplant: Field Bindweed

However, the full entry goes on to say that the only known populations of this rare moth are on the Isle of Portland and in a few specified counties in southern England. So the places to look will fall broadly into habitat category 2, provided (i) that you can find Field Bindweed, (ii) that there is some exposed soil and (iii) that you are in one of the broad geographical areas recorded.

It doesn't follow that this species will never appear anywhere else. But it is very much less likely that it will be found in a completely different habitat and a completely different geographical area. If it is, you may have made an exciting discovery. If you are sure about what you have seen, send a report to the relevant County Moth Recorder (for details see the section on *Recording and monitoring* on *page 214*).

A **Four-spotted** moth on its caterpillars' foodplant, Field Bindweed

Gardening for moths

Gardens are important places for moths. At least 41 different day-flying moths regularly visit gardens and sometimes breed. If the species of moth that fly only at night are included, this number goes up hugely. There are likely to be at least a hundred different species visiting many urban back gardens at some time during the course of a year and as many as a thousand different species have been recorded in some gardens!
If you have a garden, the way you manage it can really help moth conservation.
The habitat available for all moths and butterflies is continually reducing as urbanization and intensive farming spread, and even small gardens can attract a surprising range of moths (and butterflies).

Some moths, such as the day-flying hawk-moths, the burnets, Scarlet Tiger and Silver Y spend a lot of time drinking nectar. Encourage them to visit your garden by planting flowering plants with a high nectar content. The same flowers that attract butterflies are also good for moths. Red Valerian comes into bloom early and attracts Hummingbird and Elephant Hawk-moths. The latter is not a day-flyer but may be seen at dusk, its pink body and wings merging with the Red Valerian's blooms.

If you like buddleia, plant as much as you have space for, since it is a great favourite with many butterflies and moths (always remembering that some buddleia, including the lilac-coloured *Buddleja davidii*, can be invasive).

It is also worth establishing some areas of rough grass with native wild flowers like Marjoram, Cat-mint, Thyme, scabiouses, knapweeds, Ragged-Robin, Yarrow, thistles and clovers. If possible, it is best to avoid growing wild flowers in traditional herbaceous

The alpine garden at the Royal Horticultural Society, Wisley – a good example of a cultivated wild flower meadow

The main caterpillar foodplants of day-flying moths of gardens and parks

Foodplant	Species	Bradley No.	Page No.
Alder	Blue-bordered Carpet	1766	90
Apple	Red-belted Clearwing	379	52
Bedstraws	Green Carpet	1776	91
	Hummingbird Hawk-moth	1984	131
	Red Twin-spot Carpet	1724	77
	Silver Y	2441	168
	Yellow Shell	1742	92
Bindweeds	White Plume	1513	201
Bird's-foot-trefoils	Six-spot Burnet	169	38
Birches	Vapourer	2026	137
Cabbages	Diamond-back Moth	464	186
Cleavers	Common Carpet	1738	81
	Silver-ground Carpet	1727	78
Clovers	Latticed Heath	1894	109
	Shaded Broad-bar	1732	93
Currants	Currant Clearwing	373	46
Docks	Blood-vein	1682	71
	Muslin Moth	2063	147
General detritus	White-shouldered House-moth	648	187
Grasses	Cloaked Minor	2341	156
	Ear Moth	2360	160
Hawthorn	Feathered Bright	130	179
Horse-chestnut	Horse-chestnut Leaf-miner	366a	182
Ivy	Double-striped Pug	1862	102
Mints	Small Purple and Gold (Mint Moth)	1361	192
Nettle, Common	Common Nettle-tap	385	183
	Jersey Tiger	2067	142
	Mother of Pearl	1405	197
	Small Magpie	1376	198
Mustard, Garlic	Garden Carpet	1728	79
Oaks	Yellow-legged Clearwing	374	48
	Oak Hook-tip	1646	64
Poplar, Black	Hornet Moth	370	42
Ragworts	Cinnabar	2069	145
	Ruby Tiger	2064	144
Raspberry	Raspberry Clearwing	369a	44
Spindle	Spindle Ermine	427	185
St John's-worts	Lesser Treble-bar	1868	105
	Treble-bar	1867	104
Thymes	Common Purple and Gold	1362	193
Wall-rocket, Perennial	Lesser Pearl	1371	195

Spring nectar:
Aubretia, Bluebell, clovers, Cuckooflower, Daisy, Dandelion, forget-me-nots, Honesty, pansies, Primrose, rhododendrons, Sweet Rocket, Red Valerian and Wallflower.

Summer/autumn nectar:
Buddleia, Cat-mint, Michaelmas Daisy, Goldenrod, honeysuckles, Ice Plant, Ivy, knapweeds, lavenders, French Marigold, Marjoram, Ragged-Robin, scabiouses, thistles, Thyme, Viper's-bugloss and Yarrow.

Larval foodplants:
Alder, Apple, Aspen, bedstraws, birches, bird's-foot-trefoils, Cleavers, clovers, currants, Dandelion, grasses, Hawthorn, heathers, Common Nettle, oaks, plantains, Thyme, willowherbs and willows.

borders with rich, well-fertilized soil. As a general rule, wild flowers prefer poor soil where they are not in competition with more vigorous plants, particularly lush grasses.

Good 'old fashioned' varieties of plants are often better for moths than modern cultivars because their nectar is more easily extracted. Roses and sweet peas do not find favour with butterflies and moths! Lavenders are attractive and a good source of nectar, and sedums and Ivy blossom prolong the flowering season at the end of summer.

Not all moths are attracted to flowers. Many are less dependent than butterflies upon replenishing their energy store, and in fact some do not even have developed mouthparts and therefore do not feed at all – their plump bodies being stocked with a lifetime's food store. However, these species, like all moths, can be attracted by planting the right foodplant for their caterpillars.

The foodplants of moth caterpillars (larvae) are more varied than those of butterflies, with trees and woody plants being used by many species. Good plants to grow are Lady's Bedstraw, bird's-foot-trefoils, Rosebay Willowherb, taller grasses (ideally kept away from wild flowers to avoid choking them), thistles and knapweeds. If you have the space, Hawthorn, willows and birches are all favoured by some day-flying moth caterpillars. They will also provide a food source for the caterpillars of other moth species that become active at dusk or during the night.

The main caterpillar foodplants for the day-flying moths that are most likely to be found in gardens are listed in the table *opposite*. Some species of moth have several or many alternative foodplants, but are only listed once, against their main foodplant. The size of a garden is a key factor in deciding what to plant, but the general principle is that maximizing the diversity of foodplants is likely to increase the diversity of moths that will be attracted.

The adults of many other day-flying moths are rarely seen in gardens, even though their caterpillars' foodplants are often grown. For example, Narrow-bordered Bee Hawk-moth caterpillars feed on scabious plants (both Devil's-bit and Small Scabious), but although these plants are easily grown on a wild patch, you will usually only see this hawk-moth in the wider countryside. Similarly, the caterpillars of several day-flyers feed on heathers, but these moths are rarely seen in gardens despite their foodplants being widely grown. However, as several night-flyers that feed on heathers do come to gardens, it is still well worth growing these plants if you have the right type of soil.

Glossary

Abdomen	The rear part of a moth's body that contains its digestive and reproductive organs.
Aberration (ab.)	Of unusual and distinct appearance resulting from genetic or environmental factors.
Antenna (plural: antennae)	The sensory feeler in the head; used to detect the scent of the opposite sex.
Apex	The outer corner of the front edge of the wing.
Brood	A generation of a **species**.
Calcareous grassland	Grassy vegetation growing on chalk or limestone soil.
Caterpillar	A commonly used term for a moth (or butterfly) **larva**.
Chalk	A soft, porous form of limestone.
Chrysalis (plural: chrysalides)	A commonly used term for a **pupa**.
Cocoon	A silky case spun by the **larva** to protect the **pupa** when it metamorphoses (in some species).
Costa	The front (or leading) edge of a wing.
Dorsum	The rear (or trailing) edge of a wing.
Exuvia (plural: exuviae)	The cast-off skin or covering (usually refers to the remains left by an adult moth after emerging from its **pupa**).
Family	A collection of genera that have shared characteristics.
FL	Abbreviation for forewing length (see box on *page 12*).
Form (f.)	An alternative term used for a **race** or **subspecies**.
Frenulum	A bristle-like coupling device on a moth's hindwing that engages with the **retinaculum** to hold a moth's wings together in flight.
Genitalia	The sex organs.
Genus (plural: genera)	A collection of species that are closely related to each other.
Hectad	A 10 km x 10 km square of the Ordnance Survey National Grid.
Hibernation	The dormant stage (usually during the winter).
Imago (plural: imagines)	An adult moth.
Immigrant	A species (or moth) that arrives from outside Britain and Ireland.
Instar	The growth stage of a **caterpillar**; a newly hatched caterpillar is in its 'first instar', after it has shed its skin for the first time, it is in its 'second instar', and so on.
Jizz	The characteristic impression given by a species.
Kidney mark	The characteristic kidney-shaped mark on each forewing of many moths.
Larva (plural: larvae)	The life-stage of a moth when it emerges from the **ovum** (egg) and feeds before **pupating** (also referred to as a caterpillar).
Limestone	Sedimentary rock composed largely of calcium carbonate.
Local	The term used to describe a moth's population that is confined to a local area.
Lure	The term used for the release of an artificial pheromone scent to attract male moths.
Migrant	A species that undertakes periodic movement, usually to and from continental Europe.

Nationally Rare	Species found in not more than 15 10 km x 10 km squares of the Ordnance Survey National Grid (*page 211*).
Nationally Scarce A or B	Species found in from 16–30 or 31–100 10 km x 10 km squares of the Ordnance Survey National Grid respectively (see *page 211*).
Nectaring	Feeding on nectar.
NNR	National Nature Reserve.
Nominate (subspecies)	The reference **subspecies** when there is more than one subspecies.
Order	The **taxonomic** classification that includes, for example, all moths and butterflies.
Ovum (plural ova)	Egg.
Partial generation	The term used where some members of a species mate and have offspring while other members wait until the following year to breed.
Pheromone	The scent produced by a female to attract a mate.
Proleg	One of (usually) five pairs of stumpy legs with gripping hooks, which are towards the rear of a caterpillar.
Pupa (plural pupae)	The 'dormant' life-stage of a moth following the **larval** stage and before the **imago** (adult) emerges (also referred to as a chrysalis).
Pupation	Transformation from a **larva** (or caterpillar) to a **pupa**.
Race (r.)	An alternative term for **subspecies**.
Rare	The description of a species' abundance (implying 'very scarce').
Red Data Book	The Red List of threatened species compiled by the International Union for Conservation of Nature (IUCN) (see *page 210*).
Retinaculum	The catch on the underside of a moth's forewing that engages with the **frenulum** on its hindwing to hold the wings together in flight.
RSPB	Royal Society for the Protection of Birds.
Scarce	The description of a species' abundance.
Species	The basic unit of **taxonomic** classification describing a group of moths that can breed together and produce viable offspring.
Spiracles	External respiratory openings.
Sub-family	A collection of **genera** with similar characteristics but which are part of a larger **family**.
Subspecies (ssp.)	A collection of moths that look or behave differently from moths of the same **species** elsewhere, usually as a result of being separated geographically.
Super-family	A **taxonomic** unit describing a collection of families with similar characteristics.
Taxonomy	The science of classifying organisms.
Termen	The outer edge of a wing.
Thorax	The middle part of a moth's body, to which the wings and legs are attached.
Tornus	The outer corner of the **dorsum** (rear edge of wing).
UK BAP	UK Biodiversity Action Plan (see *page 212*).
Vagrant	A moth that has wandered outside the normal geographical range of its **species**.
Widespread	The description of a **species**' geographical distribution (which does not necessarily imply that is is common).

Moth families with day-flying species

The table below is an alphabetical listing of the moth families that include day-flying species, and the number of species that are included in this book. Each family is cross-referenced to the relevant species accounts (micro-moth families are shaded green).

Family	Types of moth	No. of Species	Page no.
Adelidae	Micro-moths (Longhorns)	1	180
Arctiidae	Footmen, tigers, ermines and others	9	139
Choreutidae	Micro-moths (including the Common Nettle-tap)	1	183
Crambidae	A diverse family of micro-moths (including the grass-moths, Brown China-mark, Mint Moth, Common Purple and Gold, Wavy-barred Sable, Lesser Pearl, Small Magpie and Mother of Pearl)	8	190
Drepanidae	Hook-tips	2	64
Endromidae	Kentish Glory	1	63
Geometridae	Generally referred to as geometrids: large macro-moths (including the carpets and the pugs)	60	66
Glyphipterigidae	Micro-moths (including the Speckled Fanner)	1	184
Gracillariidae	Micro-moths (including the Horse-chestnut Leaf-miner)	1	182
Incurvariidae	Micro-moths (including the Feathered Bright)	1	179
Lasiocampidae	Eggars	2	60
Lymantriidae	Tussocks	3	136
Noctuidae	Generally referred to as noctuids: large macro-moths (including the yellow underwings, Silver Y, Burnet Companion and Mother Shipton)	26	148
Oecophoridae	Micro-moths (including the White-shouldered House-moth)	1	187
Plutellidae	Micro-moths (including the Diamond-back Moth)	1	186
Pterophoridae	Micro-moths (Plume moths)	2	200
Pyralidae	Micro-moths (including the Rosy-striped Knot-horn)	1	199
Saturniidae	Emperor Moth	1	62
Sesiidae	Clearwings	16	40
Sphingidae	Hawk-moths	13	128
Tineidae	Micro-moths (including the Common Clothes-moth)	1	181
Tortricidae	A diverse family of micro-moths (including the Green Oak Tortrix and Arched Marble)	2	188
Yponomeutidae	Micro-moths (including the 'small ermine' moths)	1	185
Zygaenidae	Forester and burnet moths	10	28

Introduction to the species accounts

The species accounts that follow are divided into eight sections, one for each of the broad groups of day-flying moths (see *pages 14–15*). In every case there is a general introduction to the group, which includes an overview of the key characteristics of the species it includes. Within each group the species are ordered by family, and arranged as far as possible so that moths that look similar appear close to each other. As a consequence, the order in which the species appear is not strictly taxonomic, although broadly follows the widely used numbering system adopted by Bradley and Fletcher (see *page 217*). In order, the species groups are:

> **English names**
> The convention explained on *page 11* is followed when presenting the English names of all species mentioned. Plant names follow the *New Flora of the British Isles* by Clive Stace, Cambridge U. P., 2010.

A consistent approach is adopted for each species account, as explained below, and definitions of the technical terms used are given in the *Glossary* on *page 24*.

×n **English name**   *Scientific name* | B&F No. |

The English name is preceded by the magnification of the image shown. A vertical line shows the actual range in length of the forewing.
Although not all micro-moths have a generally recognized English name, those adopted by the National Biodiversity Network have been used (see www.nbn.org.uk).

The *scientific name* that is given to the species.
To the right of the *scientific name* is a box that gives the Bradley and Fletcher Number (B&F No.) for the species, which indicates its position in the taxonomic hierarchy (see *page 217*)

Legal/conservation status (see *page 210*)

Status in Britain and Ireland

Where found:	Brief summary
When flying:	month–month
Forewing length:	Range, in mm (from thorax to the apex)
Larval foodplant:	List of species

Similar species: Listed, cross-referenced to the relevant page number(s), unless that species is on the facing page

A brief description is given of the key characteristics of the species, its behaviour and life-cycle, and any unusual or especially interesting details.

For most species, information is given about the caterpillar (larva). However, it is worth noting that the colour of a caterpillar usually changes, sometimes substantially, during its lifetime. The descriptions given usually refer to mature caterpillars in their final instar before pupation. This is further complicated by the fact that in some species the caterpillars may occur in several different colour forms.

Map showing the distribution of the species in Britain and Ireland.
Distribution data are affected by factors including how well an area is recorded, and how up-to-date the records are. The maps are intended to give an indication of current distribution and are colour-coded as follows: **orange** for resident species; **pink** for migrant/immigrant species. Dark shading shows where the species is likely to occur in suitable habitat; pale shading is used to indicate where a species *could* occur even if records are few or absent, or where the species has occurred historically. Pale yellow is used to indicate where the species is likely to be absent.

Foresters and Burnets
Family: Zygaenidae

10 British species
all day-flying

Foresters and burnets are members of the family *Zygaenidae*, which has about 1,000 species worldwide. Only ten of them occur in Britain and Ireland: three foresters and seven burnets. They all have long, narrow, brightly coloured wings, often with a metallic sheen. On warm, sunny days they can be very easy to see. In late June and July you will often find the common species flying from flower to flower or mating while clinging to a grass stem. They fly slowly but with a rapid whirring of wings.

Foresters and burnets would be easy prey for birds and other predators if they were not protected by being poisonous. Both adult moths and their caterpillars can release hydrocyanic acid. Whether birds learn this from experience, or have some other way of knowing the danger of eating them is a mystery.

Despite their name, the foresters are not forest species at all. They live mostly on damp, open grassland, calcareous grassland and heathland. It has been suggested that their name derives from their colour of 'Lincoln green' of Robin Hood and Sherwood Forest fame. Two of the forester species are very locally distributed; the third, called simply the Forester, is more widely distributed in Britain and Ireland, although declining. All forester species tend to be colonial, sometimes inhabiting small areas.

In contrast, Six-spot and Narrow-bordered Five-spot Burnets are common and widespread over much of the country and may often be seen during their flight season. The Five-spot Burnet is scarcer than its close relative the Narrow-bordered Five-spot Burnet, and the other four burnet species are rarer still – you are unlikely to see them unless you happen to be in the right part of Scotland when they are on the wing.

Photographs of the eggs, caterpillars and cocoons of Six-spot Burnets are shown in the depiction of a moth's life-cycle on *page 9*. Eggs of all the species are laid in overlapping clusters on or near their foodplants, which differ from species to species. During daytime, caterpillars usually keep low in the grass until they are fully grown, when they spin a cocoon before they pupate. Most cocoons are situated low down, close to the ground, but the caterpillars of Six-spot and Narrow-bordered Five-spot Burnets have the curious habit of climbing high on a grass or plant stem before they make their cocoon. Although they can be seen easily by predators, most seem to survive. The empty pupal casing can often be found sticking out from the end of its cocoon after an adult moth has emerged.

A newly emerged
Six-spot Burnet resting
while its wings dry

A pair of mating **Six-spot Burnet** moths and a
Narrow-bordered Five-spot Burnet caterpillar
preparing to pupate (*inset*)

A **Forester** sitting on
bird's-foot-trefoil

Typical habitat of the Forester

29

×4 **Forester** *Adscita statices* `163`

This is the most widespread and commonest of the forester species, which, despite their name, live in open grassy habitats, not woodland. All three species are coloured 'Lincoln green' and there are few obvious visual differences between them. The differences lie in their life-cycles and the foodplants favoured by their caterpillars. Foresters fly in sunshine in June and July. They spend a lot of time nectaring on grassland flowers, and usually mate in the afternoon, Males are sometimes seen flying in the early evening.

Forester caterpillars feed on species of sorrel. They are whitish-green with pinkish-brown markings. Initially they burrow into the soft tissue between the skin of the leaves before moving to the outside as they mature after the winter. Then they chew the upper surface of the leaf, leaving the lower skin untouched. They tend to feed low down and pupate in the late spring in a flimsy cocoon that they spin for themselves in leaf-litter on or near the ground.

Legislative listing: NERC Act (S41 & S42)	
Scottish Biodiversity List	
Priority Species (Northern Ireland)	
UK BAP Priority Species	
Widespread but local throughout Britain and Ireland	
Where found:	Any open grassy habitat including sand dunes
When flying:	Late May–July
Forewing length:	11–15 mm ; females are slightly smaller than males
Larval foodplants:	Common Sorrel and Sheep's Sorrel

Similar species: Cistus Forester (slightly smaller), Scarce Forester (*page 32*)

Scarce Forester antenna (male)

The tips of the antennae of the very similar **Scarce Forester** are less rounded than those of the Forester

×4 # Cistus Forester

Adscita geryon **164**

The Cistus Forester is slightly smaller than its close relatives the Forester and Scarce Forester (*page 32*). The caterpillars feed on Common Rock-rose and the moths are therefore found on limestone and chalk grassland where this plant flourishes.
If you can't find Common Rock-rose in the grass, you have probably found one of the other two species of forester.

Cistus Foresters are confined to England and North Wales. They occur in small, local colonies, where they can be abundant. Although primarily a species of southern England, they are found as far north as Cumbria and County Durham.
In Wales, the Great Orme is a well-known site. Warm, flower-rich, south-facing slopes are favoured. On sunny days, look first for Common Rock-rose, and then for Cistus Foresters, which will also visit a range of other grassland flowers such as Common Bird's-foot-trefoil, Kidney Vetch and Wild Thyme.
The caterpillars, which are pale greenish with darker markings, pass the winter low down near the ground, where they eventually pupate in the late spring.

Nationally Scarce B	
Scarce but often abundant in small, local colonies	
Where found:	Open limestone and chalk grassland where rock-roses grow
When flying:	June–July
Forewing length:	9–12 mm ; females are slightly smaller than males
Larval foodplant:	Common Rock-rose

Similar species: Forester and Scarce Forester (*page 32*), although these are both slightly bigger

× 4 **Scarce Forester** *Jordanita globulariae* `165`

This is the scarcest of the three forester species, which are all similar in appearance and easily confused. However their caterpillars feed on different plants: Scarce Foresters choose knapweeds, Foresters (*page 30*) prefer sorrels and the Cistus Forester (*page 31*) feeds only on Common Rock-rose. There are minor differences in the shape of the antennae between the Forester and Scarce Forester, the latter being more pointed. Cistus Foresters are also smaller than the other two species. All three species fly in sunshine, particularly the males, and regularly perch on flowers where they are very visible. To find a Scarce Forester, look for knapweeds on chalk grassland in Wiltshire, Sussex and Kent, and then watch carefully for the emerald-green moths. But they are rare and not easy to find – and even when you do find one, it is difficult to be certain of its identity without close examination or unless you happen to see a female laying eggs on a knapweed plant. The caterpillars are pale greenish with darker markings and, like the other forester species, overwinter low down in grass. After feeding again, each spins itself a cocoon and pupates near the ground in late spring.

Nationally Scarce A	
Very localized and restricted to the south of England	
Where found:	Chalk grassland, usually with long grass
When flying:	June–July
Forewing length:	10–15 mm ; females are slightly smaller than males
Larval foodplants:	Common and Greater Knapweed

Similar species: Forester (*page 30*) (different, blunter antennae) and Cistus Forester (*page 31*) (smaller)

×4 # Transparent Burnet

Zygaena purpuralis `172`

Of the seven British burnet species, the Transparent Burnet is the most readily identified, its red spots merging together to form three distinct 'bands'. Its name derives from the fact that, as its wings are thinly scaled and the scales wear off, it becomes rather transparent in appearance.

The Transparent Burnet occurs as two subspecies: ssp. *caledonensis* in Scotland and ssp. *sabulosa* in Ireland. To find this moth, you have to visit one of its few local sites in the Inner Hebrides, on the island of Skye or the west coast of Scotland, or in and around the Burren in western Ireland. The moths fly in sunshine on flowery slopes, stopping to rest on flowers or grass stems, remaining in the open when the sun goes in, sometimes even in the rain. Their caterpillars hibernate low down in the roots of plants, starting to feed again in the spring, before spinning themselves a cocoon close to the ground. The caterpillars are brownish-green with small black-and-yellow markings.

British Red Data Book (ssp. *segontii* Endangered)

Nationally Scarce A

Scottish Biodiversity List (ssp. *caledonensis*)

Rare. Confined to local colonies on the west coast of Scotland, the island of Skye and Hebridean islands, and to western Ireland

Where found:	Mainly on steep south-facing grassy slopes near the coast
When flying:	June–July
Forewing length:	14–16 mm
Larval foodplant:	Wild Thyme

Similar species: Other burnet moths, although this is one of the more distinctive species

33

×4 **New Forest Burnet** *Zygaena viciae* `168`

This is the daintiest and smallest of the burnets. Its forewings have more black and their tips are more rounded than the other species, but these differences are small. New Forest Burnets fly less often than other burnets, and only in warm, still weather.

Unfortunately, this species has not been seen in the New Forest since 1927 and would be extinct in Britain had a colony not been discovered in Scotland in 1963. The new colony is classified as a different subspecies, *argyllensis*, but why it should occur in such a completely different environment is a mystery.

The Scottish site is a coastal south-facing slope, where the moths can often be found nectaring on Wild Thyme. Excessive grazing by sheep had reduced their population to a critically low level by the 1990s, but the situation has improved now that grazing has been much reduced.

The caterpillars are reported to feed on both Common Bird's-foot-trefoil and Meadow Vetchling. When they pupate, they spin a yellowish cocoon low down on a grass stem.

LEGALLY PROTECTED: W&C Act (Sched. 5)
British Red Data Book (Endangered)
UK BAP Priority Species (ssp. *argyllensis*)
Very rare

Where found:	Only one site on the coast of western Argyllshire; a south-facing grassy slope with plenty of low flowers
When flying:	June–July
Forewing length:	11–14 mm
Larval foodplants:	Common Bird's-foot-trefoil and Meadow Vetchling

Similar species: Other 'five-spot burnet' species (which are generally larger)

×4 # Scotch (Mountain) Burnet

Zygaena exulans **166**

Four of the seven burnet moths, including this species, have five spots. The common Six-spot Burnet (*page 38*) and the rare Slender Scotch Burnet (*page 39*) are different in having six spots (although beware that pairs of spots can sometimes be merged and appear as one). The Transparent Burnet (*page 33*) does not have distinct spots, but instead has red bands. The differences in appearance between all the 'five-spot burnets' are slight. The Scotch Burnet has comparatively smaller-sized red spots than other species, and females have little yellow marks on the shoulders of their forewings, near the thorax.

This is a rare moth confined to the eastern slopes of the Cairngorm mountains in Scotland. It occurs only at high altitude, around 800 metres. In late June and July, adult moths respond to sunshine, flying close to the ground or perching openly on low vegetation. Later in the season the caterpillars also appear when the sun is out, even in cold weather. Then they will feed (usually on Crowberry) or bask in the sunshine. When the sun goes in, they disappear rapidly into the underlying vegetation. They are green with black-and-yellow markings and pupate in late May in a cocoon attached low down to a plant stem.

Nationally Rare	
Scottish Biodiversity List (ssp. *subochracea*)	
Rare and only found locally in the central Highlands	

Where found:	Highland mountainsides
When flying:	June–July
Forewing length:	10–16 mm
Larval foodplants:	Crowberry; also heathers, Bilberry

Similar species: Other burnet moths; generally slightly smaller than most of them

35

×4 # Five-spot Burnet

Zygaena trifolii **170**

The differences between the seven species of burnet moth are all small. The Five-spot Burnet and its close relative the Narrow-bordered Five-spot Burnet are very similar indeed. The Five-spot Burnet is likely to have its two central crimson spots coalesced, but that is not always a reliable distinguishing feature. Of the two, the Five-spot Burnet is considerably the rarer. There are two subspecies: ssp. *decreta*, which tends to be found in damp grassland in many parts of England and Wales; and ssp. *palustrella*, which prefers chalk downland. The caterpillars of *decreta* feed on Greater Bird's-foot-trefoil, whilst those of *palustrella* eat Common Bird's-foot-trefoil.

It is a curious characteristic of some very similar looking moths that their caterpillars look very different or eat different foodplants. In the case of the 'five-spot burnets', the greenish-yellow caterpillars look alike but the caterpillars of the Five-spot Burnet only feed on bird's-foot-trefoils, while those of the Narrow-bordered Five-Spot Burnet eat a wide range of downland plants including vetches and clovers, as well as trefoils. This is one of the distinguishing features, and if you find burnet moths with five spots and neither of the bird's-foot-trefoils are about, you can be pretty certain that you are looking at the Narrow-bordered species.

Fairly scarce although may be locally abundant	
Where found:	Grassland, heathland and wetland, mainly in south and south-west England
When flying:	June–August
Forewing length:	14–19 mm
Larval foodplants:	Common or Greater Bird's-foot-trefoils

Similar species: Other burnet moths, particularly the Narrow-bordered Five-spot Burnet which is very difficult to distinguish

Identification is very difficult as there are no known reliable features – perhaps the most straightforward clue is that the rarer Five-spot Burnet often has the middle pair of wing spots slightly merged, whereas the widespread ssp. *latomarginata* of the Narrow-bordered Five-spot Burnet (*opposite*) only rarely shows this feature

×4 # Narrow-bordered Five-spot Burnet *Zygaena lonicerae* | 171 |

This species is very similar to the Five-spot Burnet but considerably more common. The black border to the hindwings is narrower, and the forewings are longer and narrower than those of the Five-spot Burnet. But the differences are slight. Like other burnets, they fly frequently in sunshine. Very occasionally, individuals are found with yellow rather than red markings. A number of different forms (classed as subspecies) are recognized, although the differences between these are slight: ssp. *latomarginata* is the commonest, occurring across much of England and Wales; ssp. *insularis*, found in Ireland, has more pointed antennae, narrower forewings and the middle pair of spots sometimes merged; and ssp. *jocelynae* (known as the Talisker Burnet), found only on Skye, is relatively large and also sometimes shows merged wing spots.

The caterpillars are yellowish-green with black markings. They hatch in late July and overwinter while still quite small. As they become fully grown they can often be seen exposed on their foodplant before pupating in a white, papery cocoon high up on a plant stem. This is a characteristic shared with the Six-spot Burnet (*page 38*), but not with the five other burnet species, which pupate close to the ground.

Scottish Biodiversity List (ssp. *jocelynae*)	
Common and widespread in England, Wales and Ireland; local in Scotland	
Where found:	Rough grassland and chalk downland
When flying:	June–July
Forewing length:	15–19 mm
Larval foodplants:	Meadow Vetchling, Sainfoin, clovers etc.

Similar species: Five-spot and other burnet moths

The dark border of the hindwing of a Narrow-bordered Five-spot Burnet (*inset*) is usually not as broad as that of the Five-spot Burnet

×4 **Six-spot Burnet** *Zygaena filipendulae* 169

This is the most commonly found burnet. It occurs throughout England, Wales and Ireland, but is more local in Scotland, being largely confined to coastal sites. During the day, it behaves very like a butterfly, moving from flower to flower in warm sunshine. Thistles and knapweeds are often favoured. Males patrol backwards and forwards looking for females, and mating pairs are a common sight. Their caterpillars feed on bird's-foot-trefoils, so first find these plants in flowery grassland and then look for Six-spot Burnets.

Clusters of small eggs are laid on the foodplant or nearby low vegetation. These hatch within a couple of weeks and the caterpillars grow slowly before they stop feeding to hibernate for the winter, low down near the ground. By then, they have become greenish-yellow with prominent black markings and white hairs. They emerge from hibernation and begin feeding again in the spring, and are fully grown by late May or June. Then, before pupating, they have the curious habit of climbing up an exposed stem, usually of grass, where they spin a cocoon. This is in full view of predators, and easy to see, but most seem to survive unscathed before the adult moths emerge in late June or July. There are some reports that the caterpillars may go on feeding slowly right though the year, hibernating for a second winter, but this does not appear to be usual.

Common in England, Wales and Ireland; more local around the coast of Scotland

Where found:	Flowery grassland almost anywhere
When flying:	June–August
Forewing length:	15–19mm
Larval foodplants:	Common and Greater Bird's-foot-trefoils

Similar species: Slender Scotch Burnet, which is now largely restricted to Mull, has six spots, although these are typically fused; other burnets only have five

× 4 **Slender Scotch Burnet** *Zygaena loti*

This is one of the rarest burnet moths. It is found only on the island of Mull, just off the west coast of Scotland, south of the Ardnamurchan peninsula, and on Mull's neighbouring small islands. It has six spots, although the two outer ones are often merged together, into a single, broader spot. It is slightly smaller and the wings are usually more transparent than the common Six-spot Burnet. Its name apparently derives from its dainty appearance.

This species inhabits just a few steep, grassy slopes by the sea. Formerly it was found on the Scottish mainland near Mull, but it has not been seen there for over 50 years.

Like the caterpillars of all the burnet moths, the larvae of this species pass the winter hibernating close to the ground, protected by the roots of their foodplant. They emerge in the spring, sometimes overwintering for a second winter, before pupating in May. They spin a cocoon low down close to the ground, out of sight of passers-by, not high up on a grass stem as do Six-spot Burnets.

Nationally Rare
Scottish Biodiversity List
UK BAP Priority Species (ssp. *scotica*)
Very rare; found only on Mull and its neighbouring small islands in the Inner Hebrides

Where found:	Flowery, steep, grassy slopes
When flying:	June–July
Forewing length:	11–16 mm
Larval foodplant:	Common Bird's-foot-trefoil

Similar species: Six-spot Burnet, which is slightly larger, has a bolder appearance, thicker black edges to its hindwings, and is common and widespread

Clearwings
Family: Sesiidae

There are some 1,000 species of clearwing moths worldwide, 15 of which are known to breed in the British Isles. The total number of species increased in 2007 when the Raspberry Clearwing was discovered in Britain for the first time. Another species, the Dusky Clearwing, could bring the total up to 16 if it is re-discovered, but it has not been seen in Britain for 80 years!

At first sight, clearwing moths are easily mistaken for other insects: hornets, wasps, bees or flies. The essential differences are that they have four wings instead of two, their narrow forewings have a coloured 'crossbar' about two-thirds of the way to its outer tip, and that they have comparatively smaller heads and eyes than other insects. Their antennae generally resemble those of burnet moths rather than the short, stubby antennae of bees and wasps.

Clearwings are elusive moths and until recently, before the introduction of chemical pheromone lures, the only hope of seeing one would be to chance upon it basking in the sunshine or, occasionally, flying around its caterpillars' foodplants. However, their flight is so rapid that they easily escape detection.

One of the best ways of finding clearwings is to look for the tell-tale signs of their caterpillars and pupae. Clearwing caterpillars are miners. The eggs are usually laid on the chosen foodplant and when they hatch the young caterpillars bore into the stalk, stem or trunk (whether it is an herbaceous plant, a currant bush, a Raspberry cane, a shrub or a tree). There they eat the pith, sometimes (depending on the species) for two years, rarely more, usually working downwards towards the roots. When they are ready to pupate, they make a hole to the surface before settling down just inside the hole. Adult moths emerge from these tiny holes, sometimes pulling part of their pupal casing with them. So, if an old casing sticks out, it is a sure sign that a mining caterpillar has been inside the stem, and a clearwing moth has probably emerged.

When an appropriate pheromone lure is exposed near a clearwing foodplant on a sunny day, males will often be attracted within minutes. They will buzz around the lure, sometimes settling on it or on nearby vegetation. After a few minutes, they seem to decide that there is something wrong and disappear as quickly as they arrived. By moving the lure to a new position, the process can be repeated and, with luck, some good photographs may be taken of the moths.

PHEROMONE LURES

In a few parts of the world, the damage caused by some species of clearwing moth is very serious and whole crops may be destroyed, sugarcane and maize being particularly affected. One control strategy is to lure the adult moths into traps, sometimes with a sticky surface like a fly-paper, where they are caught. To attract male moths, the pheromone scent emitted by females has been synthesized artificially, and is used to bait the traps. This sounds harsh but it is a necessary part of agriculture, particularly in India and Malaysia.

The good news is that the development of pheromone lures for agricultural pests has found a wider use, and specific lures have been synthesized for non-pest species. This has enabled clearwing moths to be seen much more easily than used to be the case.

The lure is a small rubber bung or short plastic tube that has been impregnated with an organic pheromone compound appropriate to the species of interest. This compound is volatile at room temperature and escapes slowly over two or three months if left in the open. Provided it is kept in a freezer when not in use, each lure will usually remain effective for two or three years. Such lures can be purchased from specialist entomological suppliers.

Six-belted Clearwings attracted to a pheromone lure (inside the gauze bag)

Raspberry Clearwing exploring a pheromone lure

Allotment habitat of the Raspberry Clearwing in Cambridgeshire

Six-belted Clearwing – wing structure

Six-belted Clearwing

Chalk pit habitat of the Six-belted Clearwing in Cherry Hinton

× 4 **Hornet Moth** *Sesia apiformis* **370**

Hornet Moths can easily be mistaken for Hornet wasps, being approximately the same size and having similar colouring. However, wasps have a narrow waist between their thorax and abdomen and not so much yellow on their body. Hornets have a sting but Hornet Moths are completely harmless.

The maggot-like caterpillars spend two years beneath the bark of poplar trees, usually close to the ground, and repeated infestations can kill the tree.

Although local, elusive and not often seen, Hornet Moths are quite widely distributed across parts of southern and eastern England. Pheromone lures are not always effective. The best time to look is early morning, when newly emerged moths may be found resting, or as mating pairs. Search around the base of poplar and Aspen trees in sunny situations.

Nationally Scarce B	
Found locally, mainly in parts of southern and eastern England (and formerly further north and in Wales); rare in Ireland	
Where found:	Stands of poplar trees in open sunny, situations
When flying:	Mid-June–early August
Forewing length:	17–21 mm
Larval foodplants:	Poplar trees, including Aspen, Black Poplar and Lombardy Poplar

Similar species: Lunar Hornet Moth

Hornet wasp

The yellow head readily distnguishes the Hornet Moth from the similar but smaller Lunar Hornet Moth

× 4 Lunar Hornet Moth

Sesia bembeciformis 371

The Lunar Hornet Moth looks similar to its close relative, the Hornet Moth. The differences are that Lunar Hornet Moths are noticeably smaller (if you can see the two species side by side) and their head and most of their thorax is black, except for a thin yellow collar. Hornet Moths have yellow heads.

Lunar Hornet Moths are relatively common and the most widely distributed of the 16 species of clearwing found in Britain and Ireland. However, they are not often seen and there is, as yet, no pheromone lure to attract the males. It is easier to find where their larvae have been, than to see the adult moths. This is because woodpeckers know where to look and hammer away to reach the caterpillars under the bark of willow and sallow trees. The woodpeckers leave behind tell-tale damage to the bark of the trees.

As for the adult moths, the best time to look is early in the day in July, near any species of willow where there is evidence of damaged bark, particularly where there are old pupal casings protruding from small holes.

Common but local throughout Britain and Ireland	
Where found:	Stands of willow trees in open sunny, situations
When flying:	July–early August
Forewing length:	15–19 mm
Larval foodplants:	All species of willow and sallow trees
Similar species: Hornet Moth	

Bark damage caused by a woodpecker searching for larvae

The Lunar Hornet Moth has a black head

43

×4 # Raspberry Clearwing

Pennisetia hylaeiformis 369a

This is the most recent clearwing to be discovered in Britain. In 2007, an observant gardener in South Cambridgeshire noticed signs of damage to the lower stems of his Raspberry plants, and in 2008 discovered adult moths on some nearby soft-fruit farms. Subsequently, the moth has been found over an increasing area, with old Raspberry canes on allotments being a good place to look. Males are strongly attracted to pheromone lures and usually arrive within a few minutes if they are about. After only a short time, the moths seem to lose interest and disappear as quickly as they had arrived. However, by moving to another Raspberry patch nearby, the males may be attracted again.

Heavy autumn pruning of Raspberries and the application of insecticides probably kills the caterpillars, which live inside the canes at low level. That may explain why old Raspberry patches are the best places to look. Male Raspberry Clearwings are identified by the four wide, equally spaced, orange-yellow bands towards the rear of their abdomen, and by their orange-brown tail that is fanned outwards when in flight; females only have three obvious bands.

Found locally in East Anglia and southern England but is spreading more widely

Where found:	Gardens and allotments with Raspberry patches; commercial soft-fruit farms.
When flying:	Mid-July–mid–August
Forewing length:	9–11 mm
Larval foodplant:	Established Raspberry canes

Similar species: Currant Clearwing (*page 46*) (three narrow abdominal bands), Six-belted Clearwing (*page 55*) (six abdominal bands)

Males have four wide, equally spaced, orange-yellow bands on the abdomen

Females (larger than males) only have three obvious orange-yellow bands on the abdomen

×4 **Dusky Clearwing** *Paranthrene tabaniformis* **372**

This species of clearwing may be extinct in Britain and Ireland, having been last recorded in 1924. However, that was before the introduction of pheromone lures, and it is known that these are effective in attracting male Dusky Clearwings in continental Europe. It is therefore possible that the species could be rediscovered in the British Isles. If it is, there will be no doubt about the identification. This is the only species of clearwing that does not have large clear patches on its forewings. Instead, the forewings are covered with a thin layer of dark scales, giving them a cloudy, dark appearance.

In France, Aspen, other poplars and willows are used as foodplants, as well as Sea-buckthorn. The last records in Britain were from Aspen. It seems that the caterpillars spend two winters within their chosen foodplant, sometimes making their home in old galls left by beetles before tunnelling further for a second winter. The most likely places to search will be broad-leaved woodland in southern England, but coastal sites with Sea-buckthorn are possibilities too.

Possibly extinct	
Where found:	Last recorded in Oxfordshire; all earlier records were in southern England, including sites around London and in the south-west.
When flying:	Late May–mid-July
Forewing length:	12–14 mm
Larval foodplants:	Under the bark of Aspen and possibly other poplars, willows and Sea-buckthorn
Similar species: None	

The dark, cloudy appearance of the forewings is unique amongst British species – seeing this moth in the UK would be very special indeed

× 4 **Currant Clearwing** *Synanthedon tipuliformis* **373**

This small clearwing may sometimes be seen flying around currant bushes at the end of June and is easily mistaken for a small wasp. Like other clearwings, its caterpillars bore into the pith within the stems of its foodplant. Once inside, the caterpillars, which look rather like a maggot with a dark head, spend the whole of their lives there. Before pupating, they move very close to the surface of the stem, from where the adult moth can emerge more easily.

This is one of the most widely distributed clearwing species. Males are strongly attracted to pheromone lures and will sometimes settle on nearby vegetation. The best places to look are uncared-for currant bushes in sunny corners, with Black Currant probably the most popular.

Currant Clearwing is similar to Sallow Clearwing but has two thin yellow lines on the upper surface of its thorax and a yellow collar. The Thrift Clearwing (*page 56*) is also similar but is only found near the coast where Thrift grows.

Nationally Scarce B	
One of the most widely distributed clearwings, but still classed as nationally scarce	
Where found:	Fruit gardens and allotments, mostly in England but also locally throughout Britain and Ireland
When flying:	Late May–July
Forewing length:	8–10 mm
Larval foodplants:	Red and Black Currants and, sometimes, Gooseberry plants

Similar species: Sallow Clearwing, Thrift Clearwing (*page 56*)

×4 **Sallow Clearwing** *Synanthedon flaviventris* 377

The furry catkins of Goat Willow and Grey Willow (both referred to as sallows) are a well-known sign of spring. As well as their catkins, the slender stems may harbour the caterpillars of this small clearwing moth. The Sallow Clearwing has a two-year life-cycle, overwintering twice as a caterpillar, and causing a small, swollen gall to form on the sallow stem.

This species has three narrow yellow bands on its black abdomen and can be easily confused with the similar-sized and very similar Currant Clearwing. However, the Sallow Clearwing has a dark thorax and lacks the yellow collar and two yellow lines on the thorax that distinguishes the Currant Clearwing.

The Sallow Clearwing is a rare species restricted to southern England, where it inhabits damp open woodland and heathland, wherever its foodplants grow. Males are attracted to pheromone lures, usually during the afternoon.

Nationally Scarce B	
Only found locally in southern and south-west England	
Where found:	Damp woods where sallows grow, particularly Goat Willow and Grey Willow
When flying:	Mid-June–mid-July
Forewing length:	8–9 mm
Larval foodplants:	Goat Willow and Grey Willow

Similar species: Currant Clearwing (which is the same size but has yellow lines on its thorax and a yellow collar)

The lack of yellow lines on the thorax separates Sallow Clearwing from Currant Clearwing

× 4 **Yellow-legged Clearwing** *Synanthedon vespiformis* 374

Massive Pedunculate Oak trees provide the favoured foodplant of this species of medium-sized clearwing moth. It lays its eggs on freshly cut stumps or where the bark has been damaged. The caterpillars then bore down between the bark and trunk and spend the winter hidden from view before pupating.

The adult moths are distinguished not only by their yellow legs, as their name would suggest, but by the four unevenly spaced yellow bands on their abdomens. Females have yellow tails but males less obviously so. The bushy tail of the male has black hairs above and yellow hairs below. Red scales on the central bar of the forewings of both sexes are also diagnostic. This moth is active on sunny afternoons, sometimes visiting flowers, and has a long flight season from May to as late as the middle of August in some years.

Six-belted Clearwings (*page 55*) are similar but have different habitat requirements and live in chalk quarries or on downland where trefoils and vetches grow; they are also slightly smaller and have six yellow abdominal bands, not four.

Nationally Scarce B	
Scarce, but may be under-recorded	
Where found:	Local in southern and central England and parts of Wales where oak trees grow
When flying:	Mid-May–end July (sometimes later)
Forewing length:	10–12 mm
Larval foodplants:	Under the bark of Pedunculate Oak and, sometimes, other trees

Similar species: Six-belted Clearwing (*page 55*)

Male

Red scales on the forewings are diagnostic of this clearwing species

×4 # White-barred Clearwing *Synanthedon spheciformis* **375**

The White-Barred Clearwing is one of the largest of this group of moths, identified by a single white ring around its abdomen. The antennae are unusual in having a white band along the outer half.

The Welsh Clearwing is about the same size but has two abdominal bands and a partly orange tail, which the White-barred Clearwing lacks.

This species feeds in Alder, but will also utilize birches, and is most often found on suckers and young trees. It has a two-year life-cycle (and possibly longer). The caterpillars tend to feed low down near the ground.

Look for White-barred Clearwings on heathland, mosses and damp woodland where Alder and other birch species flourish. Males are strongly attracted to lures during the middle of the day. They are scarce, but can be found locally in England and Wales.

Nationally Scarce B	
Scarce, but like many other clearwing species may be under-recorded	
Where found:	Heathland, mosses, and damp woodland with Alder and birches in south-east and central England, north to Cumbria, and in Wales
When flying:	Mid-May–mid-July
Forewing length:	12–14 mm
Larval foodplants:	Under the bark or in the roots of Alder and birches

Similar species: Welsh Clearwing (*page 51*)

The dark (rather than orange) fan tail helps distinguish the White-barred Clearwing from the Welsh Clearwing

49

× 4 **Orange-tailed Clearwing**   *Synanthedon andrenaeformis*   378

Although the Orange-tailed Clearwing is a scarce species restricted to the southern England and south Wales, it is fairly easily recognized by its bushy, orange tail. Although Welsh Clearwing and Raspberry Clearwing (*page 44*) also have orange tails, they are unlikely to be confused: the Welsh Clearwing is most similar but is rather larger and the black mark on the forewing is heart-shaped rather than squarish (the known distributions of the two species also hardly overlap); and the Raspberry Clearwing has four prominent orange bands towards the end of the abdomen.

Orange-tailed Clearwing caterpillars overwinter twice within thin stems of wild *Viburnum*, usually Wayfaring-tree, but occasionally Guelder-rose. It is probably for this reason that some populations only seem to appear in alternate years. Like most clearwings, adult Orange-tailed Clearwings are usually elusive and rarely found, but males are strongly attracted to pheromone lures, and there is the potential for more sites to be discovered. Start looking early because this species can be on the wing from mid-May.

Nationally Scarce B	
Scarce, but may be under-recorded	
Where found:	Chalk downland, limestone grassland, hedgerows and woodland edges
When flying:	Mid-May–mid-July
Forewing length:	9–11 mm
Larval foodplants:	Usually Wayfaring-tree; sometimes Guelder-rose

Similar species: Welsh Clearwing (larger, black mark on forewing is heart-shaped rather than squarish; different distribution)

Mark on forewing squarish

× 4 Welsh Clearwing

Synanthedon scoliaeformis **376**

The Welsh Clearwing is a rare and very local species. Despite its name, it is also found in Ireland and Scotland and is known from at least one site in both Staffordshire and Nottinghamshire in England.

Welsh Clearwings are recognized by their two cream-coloured abdominal bands, one more prominent than the other, and by the strong dark patch on each forewing. Females have cream-coloured outer halves of their antennae and orange tails. Males have darker antennae and brownish tails.

Their caterpillars feed below the bark of birch trees, with old Downy Birch usually being preferred. They eat the inside layer of bark and have a two-year life-cycle. Shortly before pupating, the caterpillars bore holes to the surface a metre or two above ground. Old yellowish-brown pupal casings can sometimes be found sticking out of these holes in early June, showing where the adult moths have emerged.

Males are attracted to pheromone lures during the middle of the day.

Nationally Rare	
Legislative listing: NERC Act (S42)	
Scottish Biodiversity List	
Rare and local	
Where found:	Open birch woodland and hillsides with scattered trees
When flying:	June–early July
Forewing length:	12–15 mm
Larval foodplant:	Under the bark of Downy Birch

Similar species: White-barred Clearwing (which has a dark tail fan), Orange-tailed Clearwing (smaller and with black antennae)

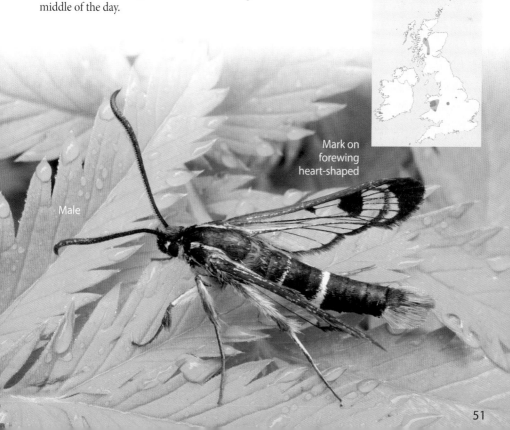

Mark on forewing heart-shaped

Male

×4 **Red-belted Clearwing** *Synanthedon myopaeformis* **379**

Apple orchards and well-established gardens are the places to look for this spectacular moth. It is a medium-sized clearwing and is immediately identifiable by the combination of its scarlet abdominal ring and black wing markings. The Large Red-belted Clearwing (*page 54*) looks similar, but is obviously larger and has red scales on its forewings close to the thorax. The Red-tipped Clearwing is of a similar size to the Red-belted Clearwing but has noticeable red scales at the tips of its forewings.

Egg-laying usually takes place in the afternoon after a fine morning and that is the best time to search for adult moths. If they are on the wing, males are usually attracted to a pheromone lure within minutes. The eggs are laid on the bark of trees and the caterpillars bore under the bark and live there throughout the winter. Infested trees can sometimes be found by finding old pupal casings poking out from exit holes.

Nationally Scarce B	
Found locally in central and southern England and in Wales	
Where found:	Apple orchards, including gardens with Apple and Crab Apple trees; sometimes in scrubby woodland
When flying:	Mid-June–late July (sometimes early August)
Forewing length:	9–11 mm
Larval foodplants:	Usually Apple or Crab Apple, but sometimes Hawthorn, pears, Rowan and Almond

Similar species: Large Red-belted Clearwing (*page 54*), Red-tipped Clearwing

The forewings lack reddish scales at the wing base

×4 **Red-tipped Clearwing** *Synanthedon formicaeformis* **380**

Red-tipped Clearwings breed on many species of willow, particularly Osier, so the place to look for them is damp, marshy ground where willows and sallows flourish. They are at their peak in mid-June but, like most clearwings, are elusive. Males are attracted to pheromone lures, usually in the afternoon, but the lure may have to be quite close to where the moths are lurking in order for the lure to be successful.

In the morning, adults can be found sitting on willow stems and have sometimes been found visiting flowers.

This species may be confused with the Red-belted Clearwing and Large Red-belted Clearwing (*page 54*) but is distinguished from both by the red scales at the tip of the forewings.

The Red-tipped Clearwing has been recorded in Britain as far north as south-west Scotland, and in Ireland.

Like other members of its family, Red-tipped Clearwings spend the winter as maggot-like caterpillars. This species overwinters under the bark of willow trees, where it lives from August to May.

Nationally Scarce B	
Found locally in Britain and Ireland and may be under-recorded	
Where found:	Damp and marshy ground, flooded gravel pits, ponds; wherever willows and sallows grow
When flying:	Late May–early August
Forewing length:	9–11 mm
Larval foodplants:	Most species of willow

Similar species: Red-belted Clearwing, Large Red-belted Clearwing (*page 54*)

The forewings have reddish tips and reddish scales at the wing base

× 4 **Large Red-belted Clearwing**   *Synanthedon culiciformis*   381

Large Red-belted Clearwings are slightly larger than their close relatives, the Red-belted Clearwing (*page 52*) and Red-tipped Clearwing (*page 53*), but their key distinguishing feature is the patch of red scales on their forewing next to their thorax. It is one of the earliest clearwings to emerge, from mid-May onwards, and is therefore on the wing before either of these species, and a good month before the Red-belted Clearwing.

The caterpillars live on Silver Birch, Downy Birch and sometimes Alder, so the best places to look for this attractive moth are sunny glades in light woodland where these trees grow. Like many clearwings, they are classed as Nationally Scarce, but now that pheromone lures are available, more sites are being discovered. They have been found locally in many places in England and Wales, and at a few localities in Scotland.

Look for them on sunny days in May and June, when the females may be found egg-laying on the bark of birch trees and, particularly, freshly coppiced birches. Both males and females visit flowers, including Hawthorn and rhododendron blossom. As with other clearwings, a tell-tale sign of their presence is old pupal casings sticking out from birch trunks, from which the adult moths have emerged.

Nationally Scarce B	
Found locally in England and Wales and in some parts of Scotland	
Where found:	Birch woodland and heathland scrub of birches and Alder
When flying:	Mid-May–late June
Forewing length:	12–14 mm
Larval foodplants:	Silver and Downy Birch, sometimes Alder

Similar species: Red-belted Clearwing (*page 52*), Red-tipped Clearwing (*page 53*)

The forewings have black tips and red scales at the wing base

Six-belted Clearwing

Bembecia ichneumoniformis **382**

×4

Chalk downs, rough grassland and quarries are the types of habitat you expect to find this smallish clearwing. With careful searching, a male may be discovered basking or a female egg-laying. However, you are much more likely to see one by putting down a pheromone lure. Then, if there are moths around, males will appear quickly.

The usual caterpillar foodplant of the Six-belted Clearwing is Common Bird's-foot-trefoil. Some years ago, a lure was tried where this plant grows behind the sand dunes on the north Norfolk coast near Cley. Prior to that, clearwings had never been noticed here; now they are found quite regularly. Caterpillars live within their foodplants' stems and a clue is to look where there are plants that are looking sickly, typically rather isolated plants on disturbed ground.

This species is rather distinctive with its obviously striped abdomen and orange scales on the forewings. Confusion is possible with the Thrift Clearwing but that species is smaller and lacks the orange forewing scales.

Although classed as nationally scarce, like many clearwings, this species had probably been overlooked before the introduction of pheromone lures.

Nationally Scarce B
Found locally in middle and southern England and in Wales

Where found:	Chalk and limestone grassland supporting the caterpillars' foodplants; quarries, cliffs, embankments, sand dunes
When flying:	Late June–mid-August
Forewing length:	9–12 mm
Larval foodplants:	Common Bird's-foot-trefoil, Kidney Vetch, possibly Horseshoe Vetch

Similar species: Thrift Clearwing (*page 56*)

× 4 **Thrift Clearwing** *Synansphecia muscaeformis* **383**

Thrift is a seaside plant that thrives in a salt-laden atmosphere. It is found all round the coasts of Britain and Ireland, on cliffs and walls, along cliff paths, on shingle and saltmarshes and sometimes farther inland on rocky areas and alongside roads that have been treated with salt. Thrift is the only foodplant for the caterpillars of the small Thrift Clearwing. This species is relatively common along the rocky coast of Cornwall and Devon, as well as being found locally more widely along or near the coastline of Wales, south-west and north-east Scotland and parts of Ireland. Sometimes, adult moths can be seen flying rapidly between flowers of Thrift or thymes, but, like many other clearwings, they are not often seen unless pheromone lures are used; then males respond rapidly if they are about.

Caterpillars feed within the stems and roots of Thrift, and foliage around the affected stems may turn brown as a result. They pass the winter out-of-sight until pupating close to an exit hole in the plant's outer skin in May. Currant (*page 46*) and Sallow (*page 47*) Clearwings look similar but are larger and are not usually found around the coast.

Nationally Scarce B	
Locally widespread	

Where found:	Coastlines where Thrift grows
When flying:	June and July
Forewing length:	6–8 mm
Larval foodplant:	Thrift

Similar species: Currant Clearwing (*page 46*), Sallow Clearwing (*page 47*)

× 4 **Fiery Clearwing** *Pyropteron chrysidiformis* 384

The Fiery Clearwing is the most colourful but also the rarest clearwing that occurs in Britain. At present, it is known to occur only at a few, predominantly coastal, sites in Kent.

This species is immediately recognizable by its orange-red forewings and bushy tail. Although there is currently no artificial pheromone lure for the Fiery Clearwing, the moths may sometimes be found flying around their caterpillars' foodplants (members of the dock family) or sometimes drinking nectar from nearby flowers. Favoured sites are usually warm, sheltered places along undercliffs or shingle banks, or above the cliffs along roads or railway track. Their caterpillars bore down into the tap root of their foodplant. The life-cycle is believed to usually take one year, but sometimes the caterpillars may pass two winters underground before pupating in time for the adult moths to emerge in June.

Although Fiery Clearwings are very rare and local in Britain, they are widely distributed (but still local) in the rest of Europe. It is a protected species that may not be disturbed without a licence.

LEGALLY PROTECTED: W&C Act (Sched. 5)
British Red Data Book (Endangered)
Legislative listing: NERC Act (S41)
UK BAP Priority Species
Only a handful of known sites

Where found:	Very local along the Kent coastline including Folkestone Warren, where they have been found since 1836
When flying:	Mid-June–mid-July
Forewing length:	9–12 mm
Larval foodplants:	Curled Dock, Common Sorrel and probably other docks

Similar species: None

Eggars, Emperor, Kentish Glory and Hook-tips

21 British species
6 day-flying

Families: Lasiocampidae, Saturniidae, Endromidae, Drepanidae

The eggar family (Lasiocampidae) has around 1,000 species worldwide, of which there are only a dozen in Britain and Ireland, and only two that fly by day: the Oak Eggar and the Fox Moth. The emperor family (Saturniidae) has about 1,300 species worldwide, but only one is native to the British Isles. And there are about 400 different hook-tips (Drepanidae) globally but only seven (one a scarce immigrant) have been recorded in Britain and Ireland, just two of which fly by day. By comparison, the family Endromidae has many fewer species: in fact, at one time it was thought to comprise only one species, the Kentish Glory, but another 21 species have since been found outside these shores.

So, from three very big families and one small one, there are only six day-flying moths in the British Isles. Or, more accurately, there are only six species of which male moths fly during the day, searching for females. The females generally keep out of sight until dusk approaches, when they take to the wing and are often attracted to light.

The eggars and the Emperor Moth are classed as 'primitive moths'; they cannot feed and rely upon the accumulated store of food and energy from their earlier existence as a caterpillar. They have broad bodies in which to carry their lifetime's supply of food. They pupate in a tough, hairy cocoon attached to grass stems or other plants, the cocoon being made from the caterpillar's hairs. The males of both these groups of moths have strongly feathered antennae which they use to detect the pheromone scent of females. If a virgin female Emperor Moth comes to a light trap and is then kept outside for the day in a suitable, ventilated container, she will probably attract several male moths to the container within an hour or two.

Although the Kentish Glory used to fly in Kent, sadly it no longer does. You now have to go to the Highlands of Scotland to have any possibility of seeing it and, even there, the chances are slim. It is now classified as Nationally Scarce A (see *page 211*). In contrast, males of the two day-flying hook-tips, the Oak Hook-tip and the Barred Hook-tip are relatively common in some parts of England and Wales, and fly around oak and Beech trees (respectively) in the daytime. Hook-tips can often be disturbed by shaking the lower branches of the trees on which they breed. Some hook-tips can feed, but they appear to do so only occasionally, and never from flowers. They may be attracted to sap that has escaped from a damaged tree or to aphid honeydew (the sticky residue left on the surface of leaves by aphids) but their tongues are too short to probe into the depths of a flower to reach its nectar.

Female Oak (Northern) Eggar

Ben Lawers: habitat for the Oak (Northern) Eggar

Endromidae: **Kentish Glory**

Lasiocampidae: **Oak Eggar**

Lasiocampidae: **Fox Moth** caterpillar

Drepanidae: **Oak Hook-tip**

Saturniidae:
Emperor Moth
(male and female
together)

×2 Oak (Northern) Eggar

Lasiocampa quercus **1637**

This eggar is called an Oak Eggar because its cocoon has the shape of an acorn. There is no specific relationship with oak trees, except that caterpillars are reported to feed on oak occasionally. Adult moths are usually encountered in open countryside. Males are strong and swift day-flyers, their large size making them easily visible, and they can frequently be found resting in long grass. The caterpillars also sometimes rest in the open, but change colour as they mature. When fully grown, they are dark brownish-grey with black rings, a broken white stripe along each side, and golden-brown hairs.

In the north, both sexes are larger and males usually have a more distinct patch of orange at the base of the forewing, next to the thorax; females are a darker brown than individuals from the south. The moths are often called Northern Eggars and are classified as a separate form (f. *callunae*), although there is no clear geographic division. In some parts of southern and south-western England, there are populations that appear more like the Northern Eggar. Northern Eggars take two years to mature, passing one winter as a small caterpillar and the next as a pupa; Oak Eggars usually mature in one year. A consequence is that adults fly later in the year in the south than they do in the north.

Fairly common and widespread	
Where found:	Moorland and heathland in the north of England, Wales, Scotland and Ireland; heathland, downland, woodland, coastal dunes, and even gardens in the south
When flying:	May–July in the north; July–August in the south
Forewing length:	25–40mm (Northern Eggars bigger than Oak Eggars; females bigger than males)
Larval foodplants:	Heather, Bilberry, Bramble, sallows etc.

Similar species: Fox Moth; also Grass Eggar (which is smaller, but not a day-flyer)

The white spot on the forewing distinguishes the Oak Eggar from the Fox Moth

×2 **Fox Moth** *Macrothylacia rubi* **1638**

This large, widely distributed moth is common in places. It is seen frequently throughout Britain and in the north and west of Ireland. For males, the predominant colours are red/brown, like a fox. Females are grey/brown (and larger than males). There are two pale, narrow bands crossing the forewings. Fox Moths are generally slightly smaller than Oak Eggars and lack the white central spot on the forewings of that species. Male and female Fox Moths behave differently: males fly during the middle of the day and at night, while females usually fly only at night. On sunny afternoons, you can sometimes see males flying about rapidly, keeping low over the ground, as they search for females.

There is only one generation a year, with caterpillars living right through to the following spring. Between June and September, they can be frequently encountered wandering over paths and tracks and on their foodplants. Initially, the hairy caterpillars are black with orange bands, but they change to become all-black except for golden-brown along their backs. They hibernate low down under dead leaves or moss, emerging in the spring, but not feeding again. Instead they form a cigar-shaped cocoon from which the adult moth emerges in early May.

Distributed throughout Britain and Ireland; common in places	
Where found:	Downland, open woods and common land, moorland, heathland, dunes
When flying:	May–June
Forewing length:	22–32 mm
Larval foodplants:	Bilberry, heathers, Bramble, Salad Burnet, Meadowsweet, etc.

Similar species: Oak (Northern) Eggar

×2 **Emperor Moth**   *Saturnia pavonia* `1643`

The Emperor Moth is large and spectacular, with a very appropriate and descriptive name. It is the only large moth to have a prominent eyespot on each of its four wings. Emperor Moths may be found anywhere, but more often in open country. On sunny days, males may be seen flying rapidly and can be mistaken for Small Tortoiseshell butterflies. Females do not fly during the day and are larger and paler in appearance. During the day, they rest in long grass, where they wait to lure an interested male by the scent they produce.

Emperor Moths fly early in the season, in April and May. Their eggs hatch by the end of May and the caterpillars feed for three months before turning into a pupa. This is formed close to the ground and is the form in which this moth passes the winter. Fully grown caterpillars are imposing creatures. They are bright emerald-green with black hoops and raised yellow spots with black bristles. Before pupating, they spin a curious silken cocoon, attached to a plant stem. The arrangement of fibres at its upper end allows an emerging moth to push through but prevents predators getting in.

Relatively common. Seen throughout Britain and Ireland	
Where found:	Anywhere with scrubby vegetation, such as heathland and moorland and open country
When flying:	April–May
Forewing length:	27–32 mm (male) 35–41 mm (female)
Larval foodplants:	Many different moorland plants including birches and sallows, Bramble and heathers

Similar species: None

Males have strongly feathered antennae, which they use to detect the pheromone scent released by females

Kentish Glory

×2

Endromis versicolora 1644

This large and beautiful moth is unmistakable. Males are slightly smaller and brighter than females and fly in sunshine or in warm, overcast weather during the middle of the day; both sexes fly together after dusk. During the day, it may be found by carefully searching the foliage of birch trees, but is now restricted to a few localities in the Highlands of Scotland where there is suitable lightly wooded habitat. The caterpillars feed on the leaves of birch and, occasionally, Alder trees, and seem to favour young Silver Birch trees on moorland, or woodland re-growth after coppicing.

♂♀

Adult moths are on the wing in April and May. The eggs are laid in clusters on birch twigs and the caterpillars, which change from black to bright-green as they mature, feed from late May to August. They spin a cocoon among leaf debris and moss on the ground, and form their pupa inside the cocoon. According to some records, the pupa remains dormant for two (or even three) winters before an adult moth emerges, the moth's complete life-cycle therefore spanning two or three years. The Kentish Glory has not been found in its original home in Kent and the southern counties for over a hundred years, and has probably been lost due to a lack of suitable habitat. Sadly, it is also becoming increasingly rare in Scotland and is now a difficult species to find.

Nationally Rare
Scottish Biodiversity List
Now found only in the eastern and central Highlands of Scotland

Where found:	Lightly wooded open ground with birch trees in the central and eastern Highlands of Scotland
When flying:	March–May
Forewing length:	27–30 mm (male) 34–39 mm (female)
Larval foodplants:	Silver and Downy Birches, occasionally Alder

Similar species: None

×3 **Oak Hook-tip** *Watsonalla binaria* 1646

Male Oak Hook-tips occasionally fly in sunshine high up around the upper branches of oak trees. Both males and females can often be disturbed by tapping the lower branches, when they will fly to a new position. They are orange-brown in colour, with pale cross lines, between which is a pair of dark dots. However, the most distinctive feature is the pronounced hook-tip to the outer edge of their forewings, which is very obvious when they are in a resting position.

Common in England and Wales	
UK BAP Priority Species (research)	
Where found:	Oak woodland
When flying:	May–June and late July–September
Forewing length:	18–30 mm
Larval foodplants:	Oaks, occasionally Silver Birch

Similar species: Barred Hook-tip (which is slightly smaller, and has a distinct dark band across the wings and usually a single, relatively faint, dark dot on the forewing)

This species is common throughout much of England and Wales, particularly wherever there are oaks in forests and woods, along hedgerows and even in gardens and parks. They may be found on Pedunculate, Sessile and Turkey Oaks, and occasionally on Silver Birch. Their yellowish-brown caterpillars have a double-pointed hump on their back, just behind their front legs. They have the curious habit of resting with their head and front legs lifted from their perch, holding on only by their rear prolegs. There are two generations a year. The pupae of both generations are formed within a spun cocoon in a folded leaf. Second-generation pupae overwinter before adult moths emerge in late spring.

×3 **Barred Hook-tip** *Watsonalla cultraria* 1647

Male Barred Hook-tips fly in sunshine and can sometimes be seen flying around Beech trees or nearby bushes between May and September. Often, they are high up among the upper branches. This species looks very similar and behaves in a similar way to the Oak Hook-tip, and is about the same size (usually very slightly smaller). However, it is generally brighter in colour, has a broad, dark band across the centre of the wings, and usually only a single dark dot in the band. A key difference, though, is that Barred Hook-tips live on Beech instead of oaks.

The life-cycle is similar to that of the Oak Hook-tip. There are two broods each year, with adults flying in May-June and July–early September. The caterpillars are also similar and pupate in a cocoon rolled in a leaf or between two leaves. Second-brood pupae pass the winter before completing their development in the spring. This species is found locally in Beech woodlands in southern England and Wales, and occasionally farther north. Sometimes they colonize isolated established trees, but stands of young Beech are also used.

Well distributed, but local	
Where found:	Beech woods in England (except the far north) and Wales
When flying:	May–June and late July–August
Forewing length:	20–28 mm
Larval foodplants:	Beech

Similar species: Oak Hook-tip (which is slightly larger and has a less prominent cross-band and darker and more distinctive dots on the forewing)

Geometrids
Family: Geometridae

300 British species
60 day-flying

The two largest moth families in the world are the Noctuidae (see *page 148*) and the Geometridae, with the order of 20,000 species in each. In Britain and Ireland, there are some 300 geometrids, of which 60 day-flyers are included. Some fly regularly during the day of their own accord, and others are easily disturbed from rest. The intention in this book is to show those species that it is reasonably possible to find if you look in the right habitat; for this reason occasional immigrants are not included.

Geometrids usually have a geometrical pattern on their wings, but that is not the reason for their name. This derives from a Greek word meaning 'ground measurer' and refers to the looping motion of their caterpillars, which move in a series of looping steps. The caterpillars hold themselves by their front legs as they lift and move forward their rear legs, making their bodies loop upwards. Then they grip with their rear legs, release their front legs and move these forward as they stretch their bodies out straight. Most feed in the open and remain on their foodplants during the day, when their cryptic colouring and 'bumpy' profile makes them hard to distinguish from a twig.

Adult geometrids can feed from flowers but seldom do so. The explanation seems to be that as they have thin, light bodies and fly efficiently, they seldom need refuelling. They settle with their wings pressed flat against the ground or whatever surface they have settled on, generally with their forewings only partly covering their hindwings. As with everything in nature, there are exceptions to the rule, and a few geometrids hold their wings above their bodies, rather like butterflies.

Different species fly in a wide range of different habitats. Several, like the carpet moths and Grass Wave, may occasionally appear in suburban gardens. Others, including the Speckled Yellow and the Orange Underwing prefer woodland and scrub. Chimney Sweepers are widespread in northern England and fly on meadows and grassy places. Others, such as the mountain moths, are rare species that can only be found in the Scottish Highlands.

The identity of many of the geometrids is usually obvious if you manage to get a good photograph of them. However, the different day-flying carpet species look rather similar, particularly if they are worn specimens. And most of the pug moths are really difficult to separate without care, whether they are worn or not. The pugs are small, some smaller than those in the group of micro-moths (see *page 176*), and have narrow forewings that they hold out sideways at right-angles to their bodies. It is therefore generally fairly straightforward to know that you are looking at a pug – but deciding which species is another matter entirely. Even experts can be uncertain without resorting to microscopic examination.

Male **Common Heath** with strongly feathered antennae – this geometrid flies in many habitats including acid heaths and moors

Speckled Yellow – a woodland species

Common Carpet – a common geometrid that is regularly seen in gardens

Lesser Treble-bar – seen in many different habitats

Brown Silver-line – flies on heath and moorland and in woodland

Bordered White – inhabits coniferous woodland and has an unusual butterfly-like pose

Chimney Sweeper – flies in colonies on meadows and moorland

Typical habitat for a Chimney Sweeper colony, Barkbooth Lot near Windermere

67

× 4

Orange Underwing

Archiearis parthenias 1661

This is a woodland moth that can be found over much of Britain, and flies in bright sunshine. It favours clearings in woodland and woodland edges, but also flies around birches on heathland. They can sometimes be seen fluttering around the upper branches of birch trees, or nectaring at sallow blossom, but they also come down occasionally to drink from puddles on damp ground. They are slightly larger than the Light Orange Underwing, which is considerably scarcer and its caterpillars' foodplant is Aspen rather than birches.

The life-cycle of Orange Underwings is determined by the availability of birch catkins. After passing the winter as a pupa, adult moths emerge in early spring and lay eggs in time for their young caterpillars to start feeding on newly formed catkins. As the catkins wither, the caterpillars move to young leaves, feeding at night. They are green with pale markings and become fully grown by the end of June. Then they pupate, usually attached to the bark. Eight months pass before the next generation of adult moths emerges the following March.

Widespread but local throughout Britain	
Where found:	Open woodland and birch scrub
When flying:	March–April
Forewing length:	16–19mm
Larval foodplants:	Downy Birch and Silver Birch

Similar species: Light Orange Underwing, which is slightly smaller, much scarcer and has slightly duller forewings (when comparing like-for-like gender)

Light Orange Underwing

×4

Archiearis notha 1662

This is the scarcer relative of the Orange Underwing, both species being woodland moths that fly in sunshine in spring. The main difference is that the commoner Orange Underwing's caterpillars feed on birches, while those of the Light Orange Underwing choose Aspen. However, the Light Orange Underwing has been seen flying around the tops of birch trees on occasion, so it is best not to jump to conclusions (on the other hand, Orange Underwing has not been seen around Aspen). Look for both species in open woodland clearings, flying around their chosen trees or drinking from puddles on the woodland floor.

Caterpillars are variable in colour, but mature to a light olive-green with two dark stripes. They feed on the foliage of Aspen, hiding in the daytime between leaves that they have spun together. When disturbed, they drop down, hanging onto a silken thread. Before pupating, it is reported that the caterpillars burrow into decaying bark or wood where they spin a cocoon of silken threads mixed with woody particles. Here they overwinter before emerging as adult moths, usually in April, although apparently some remain dormant and only appear the following year.

Nationally Scarce B	
Only found locally in the southern half of England	
Where found:	Open woodland, usually ancient woodland
When flying:	Late March to early May
Forewing length:	14–16 mm
Larval foodplants:	Aspen

Similar species: Orange Underwing, which is slighty larger and has more brighly marked forewings (when comparing like-for-like gender)

69

× 4 **Grass Emerald** *Pseudoterpna pruinata* 1665

This medium-sized moth is quite common throughout much of Britain and Ireland (except northern Scotland). It becomes grey with age as its pretty bluish-green colour fades, and can be almost white at the end of its flight period. It is readily disturbed by day, often flying short distances before settling again, and is on the wing from mid-June to August, sometimes with a partial second generation in the autumn. As its caterpillars feed on Gorse, Broom and Petty Whin, it favours open heathland and moorland, but can be found in other habitats where these plants grow.

Its caterpillars are green with pale pinkish stripes and hatch from late July onwards, hibernating during the winter before pupating in debris on the ground the following May to early June. They are well camouflaged, resembling twigs of their foodplants.

The rarer Small Grass Emerald *Chlorissa viridata* is a rather similar moth, although it is darker green and smaller. It is also easily disturbed by day and may be found around its foodplants, which include Gorse and Heather. However, it is much scarcer and, as it also prefers damper habitats than the Grass Emerald, confusion is unlikely.

Common; often frequent in England, Wales, Ireland and western Scotland	
Where found:	Heathland, moorland, waste land, vegetated shingle and some other habitats where its foodplants grow
When flying:	Mid-June–August and sometimes September–October if there is a second generation
Forewing length:	14–19 mm
Larval foodplants:	Gorse, Broom, Petty Whin

Similar species: Small Grass Emerald *(inset)*

Small Grass Emerald
Chlorissa viridata
(FL: 11–13 mm)

×4 # Blood-vein

An attractive, medium-sized moth that is creamy-white with an obvious pink fringe and a reddish-brown cross-line. When the moth is settled, this cross-line runs from forewing tip to forewing tip, continuing straight across the exposed hindwings, which are held flat to the ground. Blood-veins are often seen as they are easily disturbed from low vegetation in the summer months. Their range is spreading northwards, but they are rare in Scotland and local in parts of Ireland.

In the south of their range, there are two or sometimes three broods. The brownish-grey caterpillars feed on low-growing plants in tall vegetation in damp places such as in weedy ditches, wet meadows, woodland rides and gardens. They pupate near the ground in plant litter, where pupae from the final brood overwinter. However, the complete life-cycle of the first brood takes only a couple of months.

Legislative listing: NERC Act (S41 & S42)	
UK BAP Priority Species (research)	
Common in England and Wales; local in Scotland and Ireland	
Where found:	Damp places with tall vegetation
When flying:	May–June, July–August, September–November
Forewing length:	15–18 mm
Larval foodplants:	Docks, Common Sorrel, Common Orache, Knotgrass and probably other related species

Similar species: None

×4 # Lace Border

Scopula ornata `1687`

This very attractive, dainty moth has chalky-white wings with brown edges. These markings resemble lace, hence its name. It frequents chalk downland and is often seen flying on dry days. It rests in short grass from which it is readily disturbed. A hundred years ago, it was easy to find on the downs of southern England, but unfortunately is now scarce and very local in distribution, and may be declining further.

The best place to look is along the North Downs in Surrey and Kent, but it is also found very locally on other chalk or limestone grassland where its caterpillars' foodplants, Wild Thyme and Wild Marjoram, grow. The long, slender caterpillars are greyish-brown. There are two generations, the autumn generation coming from caterpillars that are active in July–August, and the spring generation from caterpillars that overwinter and resume feeding in the spring. Pupation occurs in a flimsy cocoon on the ground.

Nationally Scarce A	
Local in southern England; possibly declining	
Where found:	Calcareous grassland on both chalk and limestone
When flying:	May–June and August–September
Forewing length:	21–24 mm
Larval foodplants:	Thyme, Wild Marjoram, probably other low-growing herbaceous plants

Similar species: None

× 4 **Purple-bordered Gold** *Idaea muricata* `1698`

The Purple-bordered Gold is a scarce moth, but is fairly conspicuous because of its bright pink-and-yellow markings. There is considerable variation in its colouration, with individuals in the north of its range being pinker and those in the south usually more yellow. Although it mainly flies at night, this species is sometimes seen on the wing soon after sunrise, and is easily disturbed from low vegetation during the day, when it flies readily.

The Purple-bordered Gold is found only in localized colonies on damp heathland, mosses, wet grassland, marshes and fenland. It is only likely to be confused with the commoner 'purple and gold' micro-moths (*pages 192, 193*) which occur in similar habitats, but those species have darker hindwings with yellow markings.

There is one generation a year, with moths on the wing in late June and July. Their pale brownish caterpillars feed on Marsh Cinquefoil. The caterpillars hibernate during the winter before resuming feeding in the spring. In late May, they pupate in a cocoon on the ground, covered by dead leaves and other debris.

Nationally Scarce B	
Scarce and localized and restricted to scattered sites in England, Wales and Ireland; not recorded from Scotland	
Where found:	Damp heathland, mosses, fenland, wet grassland
When flying:	late June–July
Forewing length:	8–10 mm
Larval foodplants:	Marsh Cinquefoil and probably other plants

Similar species: The 'purple and gold' micro-moths (*pages 192, 193*) and another similar micro-moth, the Gold Triangle *Hypsopygia coastalis* (but that species does not fly during the day)

× 4 **Silky Wave** *Idaea dilutaria* `1704`

The Silky Wave is a rare species that is now found only at three localities. It has long been known in the Avon Gorge near Bristol, and on the Great Orme's Head in North Wales, and there is also a strong population on the Gower peninsula in Glamorgan.

This is one of several species of wave, a few of which are quite similar to the Silky Wave. Some of these species are common and others much rarer, but although they are sometimes disturbed from rest they are not really day-flyers. However, the Silky Wave is easily disturbed during the day. When found, it is easy to recognize, being quite small and having pale straw-coloured wings that are silky in appearance and have dusky cross-lines. It inhabits short, sparsely vegetated calcareous grassland usually with patches of low-growing scrub where it often rests by day.

The dumpy, dusky-red caterpillars feed on Common Rock-rose and are known to eat withered and even mouldy leaves. They hibernate during the winter, low down amongst vegetation, before resuming feeding in the spring. At the end of May, they pupate in a cocoon on the ground.

Nationally Rare

Legislative listing: NERC Act (S41 & S42)

UK BAP Priority Species

Now found only at three sites: two in Wales, and in the Avon Gorge

Where found:	Calcareous grassland and rocky cliffs with patchy low scrub and plentiful rock-rose
When flying:	Late June–July
Forewing length:	8–10 mm
Larval foodplants:	Common rock–rose, possibly also on other low–growing herbs

Similar species: Dwarf Cream Wave *Idaea fuscovenosa* and Dotted Border Wave *I. sylvestraria* (both only occasionally disturbed), and Satin Wave *I. subsericeata* (which only comes to light)

Balsam Carpet

×4

Xanthorhoe biriviata 1721

This pretty, small carpet moth was only discovered in Britain in 1951. Its caterpillars feed on Orange Balsam and Small Balsam, both of which are non-native plants that have become naturalized and grow in damp woods and ditches and alongside rivers and canals. Although still scarce, the Balsam Carpet is found in these habitats, sometimes in good numbers, and over a wide area of southern and eastern England, spreading out from the home counties into Norfolk and Nottinghamshire and now further afield. It flies in late afternoon sunshine, continuing into the evening and after dark.

There are two broods a year. The spring brood has a broad white band across its forewings, while the summer brood (illustrated) is generally darker and does not have the white band. The twig-like caterpillars may be found in June (for the summer generation) and then again in the early autumn before pupating for the winter (for next year's spring generation).

Scarce, found mainly in the south and east of England, but spreading farther north and westwards	
Where found:	Damp woodland, lightly wooded damp pasture, shady paths bordering canals and rivers
When flying:	May–June and July–August
Forewing length:	12–14 mm
Larval foodplants:	Orange Balsam, Small Balsam

Similar species: Common Carpet (*page 81*); also several other carpet species (not seen so regularly by day) have similarities, including the Wood Carpet *Epirrhoe rivata*, Sharp-angled Carpet *E. unangulata*, Large Twin-spot Carpet *Xanthorhoe quadrifasiata* and Dark-barred Twin-spot Carpet *X. ferrugata*

× 4

Red Carpet

Xanthorhoe decoloraria **1723**

Although this moth prefers to remain hidden during the day, it is easily disturbed and then flies in daylight. It is usually found on high ground in mountains and on moorland, favouring exposed rocks, on which it often settles. It is found in the northern half of Wales and from Shropshire through parts of northern England, into Scotland as far north as the Shetlands, and in the north of Ireland. There are two different-looking subspecies. The forewings of ssp. *decoloraria* (illustrated) vary from light-grey to tawny-brown with a reddish-brown central band. Those of ssp. *hethlandica*, which is found in the Shetlands, are tawny-brown with a lighter reddish-brown central band, although similar-looking examples occur elsewhere in Scotland.

There is one generation a year, with small caterpillars overwintering. These mature to become yellowish-grey with dull markings. They pupate in a silken cocoon on the ground, taking only a few weeks before the next generation of adult moths emerge in early summer. Their foodplant is Lady's-mantle and possibly other low herbaceous plants.

Legislative listing: NERC Act (S41 & S42)
Priority Species (Northern Ireland)
UK BAP Priority Species (research)
Widely distributed in north Wales, northern England and Scotland, and locally in Ireland

Where found:	**Mountain moorland and grassy hillsides with exposed rocks**
When flying:	late June– mid-August
Forewing length:	12–15 mm
Larval foodplant:	Lady's-mantle

Similar species: Other Carpet species, including the Flame Carpet *Xanthorhoe designata* (not usually a day-flyer) and Red Twin-spot Carpet

×4 Red Twin-spot Carpet
Xanthorhoe spadicearia **1724**

This is a common, small moth that is found throughout most of Britain. There are two closely spaced dark spots near the outer edge of each forewing. It has two generations in the south and has a very long flight period, being seen on the wing from April to August. Farther north, there is only one generation and the flight period is shorter. During the day, it is easily disturbed from bushes or low vegetation and then readily flies in daylight. Several different carpet species look superficially similar and it can be difficult to distinguish between them without taking a photo or capturing them for detailed examination.

The life-cycle of carpet moths varies from species to species. The short, brownish caterpillars of the Red Twin-spot Carpet grow to full-size quite quickly, especially the second generation which has to be ready to pupate in time for the winter. Their silken cocoon is made under leaf-litter or other debris on the ground. Adult moths whose pupae have overwintered do not emerge until the late spring (in the south) or later (farther north).

Common in England, Wales and lowland Scotland; local farther north and in Ireland

Where found:	Gardens, woodlands, hedgerows, downs, moors, sand dunes etc.
When flying:	April–June and July–August in the south (two generations); May–July elsewhere
Forewing length:	12–13 mm
Larval foodplants:	Bedstraws, Ground-ivy, Wild Carrot

Similar species: Other carpet moths, particularly Flame Carpet *Xanthorhoe designata* and Dark-barred Twin-spot Carpet *X. ferrugata* (both not usually regarded as day-flyers although they may be disturbed), and Red Carpet

×4

Silver-ground Carpet

Xanthorhoe montanata 1727

This is a common species throughout Britain and Ireland but is quite variable in appearance. Its central band varies considerably in width and colour and may be any shade from light greyish-brown to very dark-brown. Its behaviour is characteristic of many different species of carpet moths. During the day, it is easily disturbed when resting in grass and low vegetation and then flies a short distance before settling again. As dusk approaches, it flies of its own accord, visiting flowers, and is attracted to light, sometimes in large numbers.

The Silver-ground Carpet has one generation a year with adults flying from mid-May to July. It passes the winter as a caterpillar, pupating only for a short time in late spring. The caterpillars, which are light brown with greyish markings, feed on a range of herbaceous plants, and as a consequence this species may be found almost anywhere, particularly where there is damp, longish grass.

Generally common and widely distributed	
Where found:	Usually damp, tall grassland, along hedgerows, in woodland rides, on heathland, in gardens etc.
When flying:	mid-May–July
Forewing length:	14–17 mm
Larval foodplants:	Hedge Bedstraw, Cleavers, Primrose, etc.

Similar species: Might be confused with the Garden Carpet and Chalk Carpet (*page 86*)

× 4 # Garden Carpet

Xanthorhoe fluctuata `1728`

Some of the carpet moths are particularly difficult to distinguish without practice and the Garden Carpet is often confused with Galium Carpet (*page 80*) and Common Carpet (*page 81*). As its name suggests, the Garden Carpet is the most frequently seen of the three in urban areas, gardens and allotments, as well as being found in many other habitats over much of Britain and Ireland. Its caterpillars feed on a wide range of herbaceous plants in the cabbage family and, as a consequence, have many possible foodplants.

This is a species that pupates before the winter. There are two (or sometime three in the south) overlapping generations, each of which takes less than three months to complete their life-cycle in the summer, and about six months for the generation that overwinters. Garden Carpet caterpillars vary a lot in colour from place to place. Some may be predominantly green, others yellowish-green and some greyish-brown. They have black markings, but the head is pale. From spring to autumn, they may be found feeding at night. When fully grown, they pupate just below the surface in a silken cocoon.

Widely distributed across Britain and Ireland	
Where found:	Often in urban areas; practically anywhere except the Highlands of Scotland
When flying:	April–October
Forewing length:	13–16 mm
Larval foodplants:	Herbaceous plants in the cabbage family, such as Garlic Mustard, Shepherd's-purse, Nasturtium and cabbages

Similar species: May be confused with Common Carpet (*page 81*) and Galium Carpet (*page 80*) and possibly other carpets

×4 # Galium Carpet   *Epirrhoe galiata* 1740

The Galium Carpet is similar to the Common Carpet but the shape of the leading edge of the forewings helps to distinguish the two species. In Galium Carpet, the leading edge is noticeably concave halfway along the wing, and the forewings tend to be narrower and more tapered than similar species and have a broader dark cross-band. The colour of this moth, including the central cross-band, varies, with darker forms occurring in western Ireland and lighter forms found on chalk and limestone habitats elsewhere. Galium Carpets are less frequent than Common Carpets and have a preference for coastal locations. Like other carpet moths, they fly from dusk, but are often seen when disturbed during the day.

The long, slender caterpillars are brown with black markings. There are two generations in the south but only one further north. The caterpillars pupate in the autumn in a silken cocoon just below the ground. Like several other carpet species, they feed on bedstraws from the genus *Galium*, usually choosing Lady's Bedstraw, Heath Bedstraw or Hedge Bedstraw.

Legislative listing: NERC Act (S41 & S42)

Priority Species (Northern Ireland)

UK BAP Priority Species (research)

Fairly scarce; well localized throughout much of Britain and Ireland, but very local in Scotland; commoner around the coasts of southern England and Wales

Where found:	Cliffs and coastal areas; also chalk grassland, vegetated shingle, sand dunes and sometimes on moorland
When flying:	late May–August
Forewing length:	13–15 mm
Larval foodplants:	Bedstraws

Similar species: Common Carpet

The leading edge of a Galium Carpet's forewing is distinctly concave halfway along

×4 **Common Carpet**

Epirrhoe alternata 1738

This is a widespread and occasionally common moth throughout Britain and Ireland. Look for the dark, central crossband with a pronounced projection pointing towards the trailing edge. It occurs in a wide range of habitats, including hedgerows and woodlands, downland, heathland, moorland, sand dunes and gardens. It is frequently disturbed from low vegetation during the day and then flies readily.

There are two and sometimes three generations of this moth in the south and, as a consequence, adults are on the wing almost continuously from late spring until the autumn. However, in Scotland there is only one generation, with adults flying in June and July.

The caterpillars are variable in colour, ranging from brownish-fawn to bright-green. Those of the last generation of the year pupate before the winter in a cocoon on the ground. Like other carpet moths, the caterpillars are 'loopers', moving in a series of looping steps using their front and rear prolegs alternately.

Common and well distributed throughout Britain and Ireland	
Where found:	Almost anywhere
When flying:	Usually two generations, sometimes three in the south, May–October; one generation June–July in Scotland
Forewing length:	13–14 mm
Larval foodplants:	Bedstraws and Cleavers

Similar species: Galium Carpet, Sharp-angled Carpet *Euphyia unangulata* (which may be disturbed by day, but is rather local), and Wood Carpet *Epirrhoe rivata* (not usually a day-flyer)

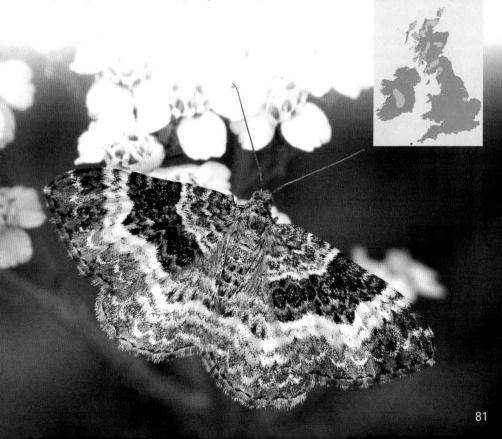

× 4

Striped Twin-spot Carpet

Nebula salicata **1753**

This rather nondescript, greyish moth settles like other carpet moths, usually with its hindwings largely covered. Its forewings have a serrated pattern of cross-lines and usually a single darker central band with irregular edges. Recently emerged moths have two overlapping dark spots in the middle of each forewing, near its leading edge, but they can be hard to see. This species favours rocky moorland, often settling on rocks, posts and tree trunks, but is easily disturbed from rest and then flies during the day.

Its brownish caterpillars are lined with white and pink, and feed on bedstraws. They are fully grown before winter and hibernate in a cocoon before emerging the following May. Their life-cycle is unusual because fully grown caterpillars remain dormant inside their cocoon, only pupating after the winter. Usually there is only one generation, although at low altitudes there may be a partial second generation.

Common in northern England, Scotland, Ireland and parts of west and north Wales; scarce in south-west England	
Where found:	Rocky moorland, other upland grassy situations, open woodland, sand dunes
When flying:	May–July and occasionally August–early September
Forewing length:	12–15 mm
Larval foodplants:	Bedstraws

Similar species: Garden Carpet (*page 79*), Twin-spot Carpet, Grey Mountain Carpet (*page 89*)

Twin-spot Carpet

×4

Perizoma didymata 1809

This medium-sized carpet moth is so variable in size and colouring that it can easily be confused with other carpet species. However, it can be distinguished by two closely spaced dark spots towards the outer edge of each forewing. Often, these spots are merged together to form a single U-shaped double-spot. Males tend to be grey, while the slightly larger females tend to be brownish or greyish-white. Males, in particular, fly rapidly on warm, sunny afternoons. This species is widely distributed on moorland, lightly wooded uplands, and along hedgerows and in light woodland on lowland sites and, occasionally, is seen in numbers.

There is one generation. Although the female lays her eggs in late summer, they have to survive the winter and do not hatch until the following spring. The caterpillars, which are yellowish-green, feed from April to June on many different plants, including Bilberry, Heather and Cow Parsley. Like many other carpet species, some of the moths on offshore islands look different and those on the Shetlands have been given subspecies status. This subspecies, *hethlandica,* has more muted colours than those found elsewhere.

Common, particularly in the west and north of Britain and in Ireland; seen less frequently in the south and south-east of England

Where found:	Many different habitats, woodland, hedgerows, moorland, sand dunes, sea-cliffs, gardens
When flying:	June–August
Forewing length:	11–15 mm
Larval foodplants:	Bilberry, Heather, sallows, Greater Stitchwort, Cow Parsley, etc.

Similar species: Garden Carpet (*page 79*) and Striped Twin-spot Carpet

Small Argent and Sable

×4

Epirrhoe tristata **1737**

Not so dashing and colourful as its larger relation the Argent and Sable, this dainty carpet moth is a variable species, with grey-brown or brownish markings; its central dark band can be broad or narrow and, although usually continuous, is sometimes divided. Unless you can take a good photograph or catch the moth for close inspection, definite identification may be difficult as there are several carpet moths of similar size.

The Small Argent and Sable can be quite common in parts of Scotland, often flying on sunny afternoons and as dusk approaches. Sometimes, hundreds may be seen on the wing together. It is absent from, or uncommon in, much of Britain and Ireland, although some large colonies exist on high ground. There is one generation a year except in south-west England and in southern Ireland, where there may be a partial second brood. The caterpillars, which are grey-brown with darker markings, feed on Heath Bedstraw from late June into the autumn, pupating before the winter in a cocoon on the ground.

Common in Wales, Scotland and parts of northern England; occasional elsewhere, particularly in south-west England and in Ireland.

Where found:	High moorland, high limestone grassland, upland woodlands and hedgerows
When flying:	Late May–early July, sometimes August
Forewing length:	11–13 mm
Larval foodplant:	Heath Bedstraw

Similar species: Garden Carpet (*page 79*), Galium Carpet (*page 80*), Argent and Sable

The Small Argent and Sable usually has a continuous dark central band across the forewing, distinguishing it from the larger Argent and Sable

×4 **Argent and Sable** *Rheumaptera hastata* `1787`

The Argent and Sable is easy to recognize by its striking black-and-white markings. It is much less common than it was fifty years ago, and is now extremely local in southern England and the west Midlands. Scottish moorlands and the west of Ireland are the best places to look. There are two subspecies: the nominate subspecies, whose size and intensity of markings may vary, and ssp. *nigrescens* that is smaller. The latter may have brownish-black or greyish-black markings, but also shows considerable variation.

In southern woodland sites, search in the vicinity of birch trees to find adults flying during the day. Eggs are usually laid on the leaves of birch saplings. In northern England, Wales, Scotland and Northern Ireland, Bog-myrtle may be preferred, although birches and sometimes sallows are also used as foodplants. The dark, blackish-green caterpillars spin together leaves to form a home for themselves, and feed from June to August (or later in the north). They crawl down to the ground to pupate in leaf-litter in the autumn, with adult moths emerging by the start of May.

Nationally Scarce B	
Legislative listing: NERC Act (S41 & S42)	
Scottish Biodiversity List	
Priority Species (Northern Ireland)	
UK BAP Priority Species	
Widespread but local in Britain and Ireland; commonest on the Scottish moors	
Where found:	Open woodland, moorland and bogs
When flying:	May to July, usually earlier in the south
Forewing length:	13–19mm
Larval foodplants:	Foliage of birch trees (Downy Birch and Silver Birch) and Bog-myrtle, occasionally sallows

Similar species: Small Argent and Sable

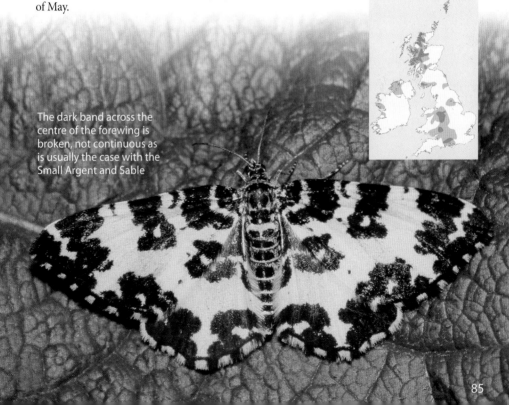

The dark band across the centre of the forewing is broken, not continuous as is usually the case with the Small Argent and Sable

× 4 **Chalk Carpet** *Scotopteryx bipunctaria* `1731`

The Chalk Carpet can be distinguished from the other carpet moths by the two tiny black spots in the middle of the top edge of each forewing and by its chalky-grey colour. There is not much variation except for a slightly darker central cross-band. Its forewings are quite pointed.

This species is scarce but occurs locally over much of southern England and parts of Wales on chalk grassland and in old quarries, often resting on open patches of soil or chalk from which it is easily disturbed and flies readily during the day.

The caterpillars are whitish-brown, lined with grey and with black dots. They feed at night on trefoils and clovers, and have a long growing season, from August through to the following June. Then they pupate for only a short period, in a cocoon on or just below the ground, before adult moths emerge in July.

Nationally Scarce B	
Legislative listing: NERC Act (S41 & S42)	
UK BAP Priority Species	
Found locally in southern England and parts of south Wales and as far north as Cumbria and Northumberland	
Where found:	Calcareous grassland, chalk quarries, coastal cliffs with some bare soil
When flying:	July–August
Forewing length:	15–18mm
Larval foodplants:	Trefoils, clovers, vetches
Similar species: None	

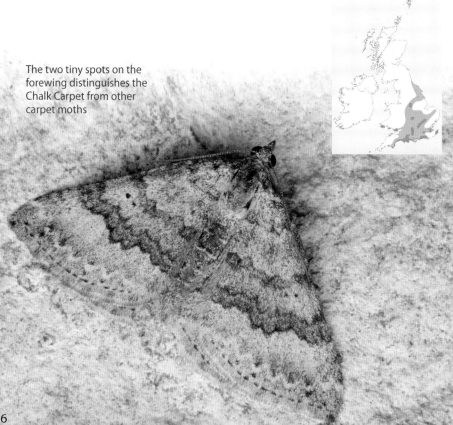

The two tiny spots on the forewing distinguishes the Chalk Carpet from other carpet moths

×4 **White-banded Carpet**   *Spargania luctuata*   1786

This is a scarce carpet moth that was first discovered in south-east England in 1924. It was probably an immigrant species but has since established itself in Kent, Sussex and parts of East Anglia. It can be recognized by the distinctive irregular, broad, white band across its blackish-brown forewings. The hindwings are mainly white with a dark border. As well as flying on sunny afternoons, this species is readily disturbed from rest in low vegetation in woodland rides and clearings. Its preferred habitat is open areas of woodland where Rosebay Willowherb is growing.

There are usually two generations a year (although the second may only be a partial generation), with caterpillars growing quickly and taking about six weeks to reach maturity in June–July or August–September. The caterpillars have two colour forms and may be either mainly brown or mainly green. When fully grown, they pupate on the ground, where they remain until the new generation emerges the following May.

Nationally Scarce A	
Mainly in south-eastern England, although there are occasional records from further afield	
Where found:	Wide rides and open areas in woodland
When flying:	Mid-May–mid-June and mid-July–August
Forewing length:	14–15 mm
Larval foodplants:	Rosebay and possibly other willowherbs

Similar species: Cloaked Carpet *Euphyia biangulata* and Sharp-angled Carpet *Epirrhoe unangulata*, but these do not have such a dark outer band to their wings and are not usually seen by day

× 4 # Yellow-ringed Carpet

Entephria flavicinctata **1743**

The Yellow-ringed Carpet is a nationally scarce moth which has very restricted sites. It favours rocky locations and often settles on steep rock faces. If it is disturbed, it flies readily during the day before settling again. There may be one or two generations a year, but usually only one at inland sites. It often flies alongside the Grey Mountain Carpet, which looks similar except that it has no trace of the orange or gold that characterizes the Yellow-ringed Carpet.

There are two subspecies: ssp. *flavicinctata* (illustrated) has golden-orange central stripes on a pale background, whereas ssp. *ruficinctata* is altogether darker and without such obvious central stripes and colouring. Usually, ssp. *flavicinctata* has two generations a year, flying in May and August, while ssp. *ruficinctata* has only one generation, flying in July to early August. Both subspecies pass the winter as dull, bristly caterpillars of variable colour. These eat the flowers of their foodplant and then pupate for a few weeks in a cocoon wedged in a rocky crevice in late spring or early summer.

Nationally Scarce B	
Priority Species (Northern Ireland)	
Very local, mainly in western Scotland, Yorkshire and Northern Ireland, but also found in North Wales, the Black Mountains, Brecon and formerly in Cumbria	
Where found:	Usually rocky limestone moorland, quarries and ravines
When flying:	May and July–August
Forewing length:	17–18 mm
Larval foodplants:	Mossy, Yellow or Purple Saxifrage, English Stonecrop

Similar species: Grey Mountain Carpet

× 4 **Grey Mountain Carpet** *Entephria caesiata* 1744

The Grey Mountain Carpet is a relatively common moth of high moorland and rocky mountain habitats, being found in northern England, parts of Wales and in Scotland, where it can occasionally be seen in numbers. This species also occurs widely in Ireland, although only locally. It often rests on exposed rocks and stone walls, as well as on vegetation, from where it is easily disturbed.

There are two other day-flying carpet species that occur in similar habitats and may be found with the Grey Mountain Carpet: the Striped Twin-spot Carpet (*page 82*), which is smaller, and the much scarcer Yellow-ringed Carpet. The Grey Mountain Carpet can be distinguished from the Yellow-ringed Carpet by the fact that the wings' central band is usually quite dark, without any hint of yellow.

There is one generation a year. The caterpillars, which are usually green, with brown-and-yellow markings, eat heathers and Bilberry from late summer and throughout the winter. In early summer, they pupate in a cocoon on the ground among leaf-litter.

Legislative listing: NERC Act (S41 & S42)
Priority Species (Northern Ireland)
UK BAP Priority Species (research)
Common in mountainous areas

Where found:	High ground, mainly in the north of England, Wales, Scotland and Ireland
When flying:	Late June–early October, with the flight period starting later in the north
Forewing length:	16–19 mm
Larval foodplants:	Heather and Bilberry

Similar species: Striped Twin-spot Carpet (*page 82*), Yellow-ringed Carpet

× 4

Blue-bordered Carpet

Plemyria rubiginata 1766

The attractive Blue-bordered Carpet is a fairly common moth and can be found almost anywhere. It occurs as two subspecies in the British Isles. The most widespread is ssp. *rubiginata* (illustrated), which occurs in England, Wales and Ireland, and favours damp meadows and woodlands (including gardens and country lanes). Its forewings have a blue-grey outer border. In the more local ssp. *plumbata*, which flies in the north of England and lowland Scotland, the central bar stretches right across the forewings and the outer border is darker. There is also a dark form f. *semifumosa* (often seen in ssp. *plumbata*) in which the chalky-white colouration is replaced by pale grey-brown.

Although widespread, the Blue-bordered Carpet usually only occurs in small numbers. It flies in late afternoon, continuing through the evening and after dark.

The long, thin, green caterpillars feed on woody plants, particularly Blackthorn and Alder. This carpet species is unusual in that it passes the winter as an egg, laid in late summer in the fork of a tree or a bush. The eggs do not hatch until April and the pupal stage only lasts for a short time in early summer. There is only one generation.

Fairly common, except in northern Scotland, but typically local and found in small numbers	
Where found:	Damp habitats including woodland, scrub, hedgerows and gardens
When flying:	Late May–August
Forewing length:	12–15 mm
Larval foodplants:	Blackthorn, Alder, birches and other trees

Similar species: None

×4 **Green Carpet** *Colostygia pectinaria* `1776`

This small moth is common throughout Britain and Ireland, and starts life with a greenish tinge but rapidly loses the green to become yellowish-white. The arrangement of dark patches, with two on the leading edge and one on the trailing edge of the forewing, is diagnostic, even when the moth is badly faded.

It may be found in gardens, road verges, hedgerows, open woodland and heathland at almost any altitude, including high moorland, wherever bedstraws occur.

Green Carpets are often disturbed from rest during the day, but generally fly in the late afternoon and after dark.

The caterpillars are bristly olive-brown which, like many other carpet species, feed on bedstraws. They overwinter and eventually pupate in a cocoon on the ground in May. In the south, there are two generations.

Common and widespread	
Where found:	Many different habitats, including heathland, moorland, open woodlands, hedgerows, gardens
When flying:	May–mid-July and August–September in the south; June–August in northern Britain
Forewing length:	12–15 mm
Larval foodplants:	Hedge Bedstraw, Heath Bedstraw, probably Cleavers; possibly other low-growing plants

Similar species: None

×4

Yellow Shell

Camptogramma bilineata `1742`

This is an attractive, medium-sized carpet moth that occurs in many different habitats in Britain and Ireland. Its colour and size are quite variable and there are several different forms, many of which are named as subspecies. This species prefers lowland sites inland and is seldom found on high moorland. Look for the Yellow Shell close to the ground at the base of hedges and fences, from where it may be disturbed during the day. It is often on the wing as dusk approaches, when it may be seen visiting flowers.

Although primarily inland moths, Yellow Shells can also occur on coastal habitats, including rocky cliffs in northern Scotland and the Hebrides, as well as off the coast of south-west Ireland. These are all darker than those found in other habitats.

There is only one generation a year, with the stout, yellowish-green caterpillars feeding from August to May on a range of low-growing herbaceous plants including Cleavers and other bedstraws. They pupate on the ground in loose earth under their foodplant.

Widely distributed and occasionally seen in numbers throughout Britain and Ireland	
Where found:	Mainly lowland sites, including hedgerows, gardens, damp fenland, and riverbanks; also rocky coasts and cliffs.
When flying:	Late May–August
Forewing length:	13–16 mm
Larval foodplants:	Cleavers, other bedstraws, docks, wormwoods, chickweeds, sorrels, etc.

Similar species: None

Dark form from the Outer Hebrides, probably ssp. *atlantica*

×4 # Shaded Broad-bar *Scotopteryx chenopodiata* **1732**

The Shaded Broad-bar is easily disturbed from long grass and low vegetation where it rests during the day. It is distinctive, with a central broad band composed of parallel narrower bands of varying shades of brown, and usually has a short, dark diagonal stripe in the tip of its forewings. However, like many of the Geometridae family, its colours are variable. It is a common species that may be found in open, grassy places all over Britain and Ireland, except on very high ground.

Its caterpillars, which are predominantly greyish-brown, although with different coloured markings, feed on vetches and clovers from September right through to the following June. Then they pupate for just a few weeks before the next generation of adult moths emerge. The Shaded Broad-bar is a nectar-drinking moth, feeding at flowers, but usually does so only at night. It was once called the Small Mallow because of its resemblance to the Mallow moth *Larentia clavaria*, but that is not a day-flying species and is seen only occasionally if it is attracted to light.

Legislative listing: NERC Act (S41 & S42)

Priority Species (Northern Ireland)

UK BAP Priority Species (research)

Common throughout much of Britain and Ireland except the Highlands of Scotland

Where found:	Grassy habitats, including downland, woodland rides, hedgerows, roadside verges and sometimes suburban gardens
When flying:	June–September
Forewing length:	16–19 mm
Larval foodplants:	Vetches and clovers

Similar species: Mallow *Larentia clavaria* (but this is larger, rarely seen during the day, and only flies from late September to November)

× 4

Lead Belle

Scotopteryx mucronata **1733**

The name of this species well describes its background-colour, which is that of a weathered lead roof. It is very similar to the July Belle, but a distinguishing feature is the dark spot roughly in the middle and near the leading edge of each forewing. In the Lead Belle this is usually shaped like a tadpole, whereas in the July Belle it tends to be much more circular and closer to the second cross-line than the third. However, perhaps the most helpful method of identification is to note what time of year you see one. If in May, you are almost certainly looking at a Lead Belle; if in July and early August, it is more probably a July Belle (although the two species do overlap for some weeks in June). The Lead Belle has two subspecies: ssp. *umbrifera* (illustrated) in south-west England and south Wales, and the darker ssp. *scotica* farther north and in Ireland.

Both Lead Belle and July Belle are easily disturbed from rest on their food plants (both use Gorse, Dyer's Greenweed and Petty Whin), and then fly before settling again. The long, rather stout caterpillars of the Lead Belle are yellowish-brown with darker-brown markings. There is one generation a year, and they continue to feed in mild weather throughout the winter. They pupate in the spring in a cocoon attached to their foodplant or in leaf litter on the ground.

Widespread in south-west and northern England, Wales, Scotland and Ireland	
Where found:	Grassy heathland, moorland, sometimes other scrubby situations
When flying:	mid-May– mid-June
Forewing length:	15–19 mm
Larval foodplants:	Gorse, Broom, Petty Whin, Dyer's Greenweed

Similar species: July Belle

×4 **July Belle** *Scotopteryx luridata* 1734

July Belle is very similar to Lead Belle, and the two species can be hard to separate. A fairly reliable distinguishing feature is that July Belle has only a faint darkish dot in the middle of each forewing, near the leading edge and closer to the second cross-line than the third, whereas Lead Belle has larger, darker and more irregularly shaped dots.

Caterpillars of both species feed on Gorse, Petty Whin, Dyer's Greenweed and probably also Broom. Adult moths are often disturbed from these foodplants and then fly during the day. However, their flight periods are different, with July Belle, as its name suggests, being on the wing in July (though also occurring slightly earlier and later in the year), and the Lead Belle flying from mid-May to mid-June.

The July Belle is more widespread than the Lead Belle, although still only found locally. It occurs in much of Britain and Ireland in many different habitats and, occasionally, may be seen in numbers. As well as heathland and moorland, its habitats include open woodland and even shingle beaches. There is one generation a year and the caterpillars, which are pale brown with a bluish tinge, overwinter, pupating in early summer on or near their foodplant.

Widespread but local throughout Britain and Ireland	
Where found:	Scrubby heathland and moorland, downland, open woodland, shingle beaches
When flying:	Mid-June–early August
Forewing length:	15–19 mm
Larval foodplants:	Gorse, Petty Whin and Dyer's Greenweed

Similar species: Lead Belle

× 4 **Heath Rivulet** *Perizoma minorata* `1805`

Heath Rivulets are found very locally in Scotland, on high moorland in Cumbria and the Pennines, and in Ireland, both from the north-east and from the Burren. Although small, they are quite distinctive moths that fly on sunny afternoons in mid-summer. This species may be declining, but it is possibly under-recorded. There are two similar day-flyers: the Pretty Pinion, which has a more dappled and contrasting wing pattern, and occurs predominantly in Scotland; and the Grass Rivulet (*page 98*), which is lighter in colour and slightly larger. Both also fly in the afternoons.

The Heath Rivulet has one generation a year, with moths flying towards the end of the summer in July and August. Their pale-green caterpillars feed on the flowers and developing seeds of Eyebright, and are fully grown by the end of September. They pupate low down in underground cocoons from which adult moths emerge nine months later during the following July.

Nationally Scarce B	
Very local in upland Scotland; rare elsewhere in northern England and Ireland	
Where found:	Moorland, upland pasture and limestone grassland
When flying:	July–August
Forewing length:	8–10 mm
Larval foodplants:	Flowers and seeds of Eyebright

Similar species: Grass Rivulet (*page 98*) and Pretty Pinion, but these both fly earlier, starting in May

A well-marked Heath Rivulet (*left*) and a less well-marked individual (*right*) that resembles a Pretty Pinion

×4 **Pretty Pinion**   *Perizoma blandiata* 1806

This pretty little moth is quite local. Like the Heath
Rivulet, it is mainly confined to Scottish moorland
and the Burren in Ireland, but there are records
from Cumbria and the Wye and Severn Valleys.
Look for the broad band that runs across the
middle of its forewings. This is solid grey at the
leading edge but fades towards the middle before
becoming darker grey again approaching the
trailing edge. On islands off the western coast of
Scotland ssp. *perfasciata* occurs. This subspecies
is darker and with a more uniform central band
than those found elsewhere.

There is one generation, with adults on the wing
from late May to early August (earlier than the
Heath Rivulet, but overlapping). The adult moths
usually fly in the late afternoon. A range of different
habitats are favoured, from areas of tall grass with
the larval foodplant, Eyebright, to areas of short turf.
Caterpillars are green with crimson-and-pink markings.
They feed on the flowers and seeds of Eyebright, rather
than its leaves. Before the winter, they pupate in a
cocoon on the ground.

Priority Species (Northern Ireland)	
Local, mainly in northern Scotland and the Burren region of Ireland	
Where found:	Open moorland, pasture, roadside verges, track edges
When flying:	May–early August
Forewing length:	9–11 mm
Larval foodplant:	Eyebright

Similar species: Heath Rivulet (which flies
later, although the flight periods overlap),
Grass Rivulet (*page 98*) (larger and
lighter), and Lime-speck Pug *Eupithecia
centaureata*, but that species is not usually
seen by day

×4 # Grass Rivulet

Perizoma albulata 1807

The Grass Rivulet is a small, whitish moth that is more lightly patterned than two similar species, the Heath Rivulet (*page 96*) and Pretty Pinion (*page 97*). Its often chalky-white forewings have brownish bands running across them but they do not have the intensity of colour of the other two species. On Shetland, a darker ssp. *subfasciaria* is found.

As its name suggests, this is a grassland species and it may be found almost anywhere, although colonies can be very local. It flies by day, usually in the late afternoon, and sometimes large numbers can be seen on the wing together.

There is one generation a year. Whereas caterpillars of the two similar species feed on the developing seeds of Eyebright, Grass Rivulet caterpillars feed on the seeds of Yellow-rattle. They are greenish-white and live hidden inside the seed capsules, crawling down to the ground to spin a cocoon on or below the surface. Here they spend the winter, and emerge as adult moths in May.

Widespread but local	
Where found:	Grassland, often calcareous, also sand dunes and vegetated shingle
When flying:	May–early July
Forewing length:	10–12 mm
Larval foodplant:	Yellow-rattle

Similar species: Heath Rivulet (*page 96*), Pretty Pinion (*page 97*)

A pale Grass Rivulet (*left*) can look quite different from a typically marked individual (*right*)

× 4 **Slender-striped Rufous** *Coenocalpe lapidata* **1780**

The Slender-striped Rufous is a scarce and very local day-flying moth. It is confined to moorland sites, and usually areas where damp flushes with rushes occur.

The best time to see one is on warm, sunny afternoons, when they can occasionally be found in numbers. However, as soon as the sun goes in they disappear to hide in the vegetation. Their sandy colour and light hindwings, which are exposed when they settle, are straightforward identification features, but it is quite possible that the species is under-recorded. There are prominent narrow, dark, wavy lines across their forewings. Females tend to be paler and slightly smaller than males.

There is one generation, with adults on the wing in the autumn. Like other late-season moths, they overwinter in the egg stage, usually attached low down to a plant stem. The eggs hatch the following April and when the caterpillars are fully grown in early August they are pale buff with grey markings. They pupate in a cocoon which they spin in loose soil on the ground.

Nationally Scarce A	
Only scattered sites in central and northern Scotland, and in Ireland	
Where found:	Rough, usually damp, upland pasture and open moorland
When flying:	September–early October
Forewing length:	13–16 mm
Larval foodplants:	Probably Meadow Buttercup
Similar species: None	

99

× 4 # Marsh Pug

Eupithecia pygmaeata **1822**

There are many different pug species, some of which can be disturbed by day, but there are only a few that fly regularly in daylight, of which the Marsh Pug is one. This is a very small, dark-brown moth that, like all species of pug, rests with its wings stretched out sideways. Although it is superficially similar to many other pugs, look for the straight leading edge to its forewing. On sunny afternoons in early summer, it is occasionally seen in numbers fluttering around the flowers of Field Mouse-ear, the larval foodplant. The usual habitat is marshy ground or, sometimes, vegetated sand dunes or the damp slacks on their landward side. However, the Marsh Pug is a scarce moth, and although it is found throughout Britain and Ireland, the sites at which it occurs are widely scattered.

There is one generation a year. The long, thin, yellowish-green caterpillars feed during June and July before pupating, probably on the ground, where they overwinter until the adult moths emerge the following summer.

Nationally Scarce B	
Scattered distribution across Britain and Ireland; rare in the south	
Where found:	Marshy ground, damp meadows, fenland, sand-dunes and waste ground
When flying:	May–June
Forewing length:	8–9 mm
Larval foodplants:	Flowers and seed capsules of Field Mouse-ear and possibly other mouse-ears

Similar species: Double-striped Pug (*page 102*) (much more common)

×4 Satyr Pug

Eupithecia satyrata 1828

Although a small moth, the Satyr Pug is the largest of the three pug species included in this book that most often fly during the day. Its forewings are light fawn in colour with closely spaced, thin, irregular brown bands (which show more clearly on some individuals than others). Three different subspecies are recognized: ssp. *satyrata* (illustrated) is found on lowland sites; ssp. *callunaria*, which is smaller and darker, on northern upland sites; and ssp. *curzoni*, with bolder markings, on Shetland (some forms on Orkney also resemble this subspecies). On warm, still days on upland sites, Satyr Pugs sometimes fly in numbers in late afternoon, although for some reason this is less likely to happen in lowland locations.

The caterpillars are variable in colour but are generally greenish, with brown-and-yellow markings. They are not at all fussy about their foodplant, and eat the flowers of many different moorland plants such as Heather, Cross-leaved Heath, Meadowsweet, knapweeds and Devil's-bit Scabious. By the end of September, they have pupated for the winter. There is only one generation a year.

Widespread but local, mainly in northern England, Scotland and Ireland; scarcer in Wales and southern England	
Where found:	Upland grassland and moorlands; also on chalk downland, heathland, fens, waste ground and open woodland
When flying:	May–June
Forewing length:	9–13 mm
Larval foodplants:	Flowers of many different plants, including heathers, Meadowsweet, knapweeds

Similar species: Marsh Pug and Double-striped Pug (*page 102*) (smaller)

×4 **Double-striped Pug** *Gymnoscelis rufifasciata* 1862

The Double-striped Pug is the commonest and most widespread of the three pug species that habitually fly during the day. It always settles with its forewings stretched out and its hindwings showing – the pose that is typical of all pug species. It is very small and variable in size and colour but, for a pug, fairly distinctively marked, with two irregular stripes across its wings. It sometimes flies in hot sunshine, stopping to visit flowers. By tapping bushes, adults can be disturbed almost anywhere. Except in northern Britain, there are usually two generations and, in the south of England, there are sometimes three. The Double-striped Pug is usually on the wing by late March and may be seen flying as late as October.

The caterpillars are variable in colour, ranging from yellowish-olive to reddish-brown, with different coloured markings. They eat the flowers of both woody and some herbaceous plants. Caterpillars pupate before the start of winter, usually under plant debris on the ground.

Common and widely distributed throughout Britain and Ireland	
Where found:	A wide range of habitats, including heathland, moorland, woodlands, hedgerows, parks, gardens
When flying:	Late March–May and July–August, sometimes into October if there is a third brood in the south; mid-May–July in northern Britain
Forewing length:	8–10 mm
Larval foodplants:	Ivy, Gorse, heathers and many other plants

Similar species: Marsh Pug (*page 100*), Satyr Pug, which is slightly larger (*page 101*) and Juniper Pug *Eupithecia pusillata*, which occasionally may be found near Juniper plants in July–September sunshine.

This species is quite variable in size and appearance.

×4 **Manchester Treble-bar** *Carsia sororiata* `1866`

Manchester Treble-bars are attractive small moths and, as the name suggests, are a northern species. They live on the low vegetation of damp moors, peat bogs and raised mosses. Although they naturally fly at the end of the day, they are easily disturbed from low vegetation and then fly during the daytime.

They are similar in appearance to the Treble-bar (*page 104*) and Lesser Treble-bar (*page 105*), although more colourful and smaller than both those species. The Manchester Treble-bar overwinters as an egg, its caterpillars eat the flowers and leaves of various woody shrubs, and it has just one generation a year. This is very different from the other two treble-bars which have two generations over much of their range, hibernate as caterpillars, and eat only St John's-worts (herbaceous plants in the genus *Hypericum*). Although the caterpillars of the three treble-bars are similar in size and shape, their colours and markings vary.

Nationally scarce B	
Restricted to the north of England, Scotland and Ireland	
Where found:	Peat bogs, mosses, damp moorland
When flying:	July–August
Forewing length:	11–15 mm
Larval foodplants:	Bilberry, Cranberry, Cowberry

Similar species: Treble-bar (*page 104*) and Lesser Treble-bar (*page 104*)

× 4 **Treble-bar** *Aplocera plagiata* `1867`

The Treble-bar and Lesser Treble-bar are two very similar members of the family Geometridae. It is almost impossible to distinguish the two species without examining them under a microscope and looking at the shape of the tip of the abdomen (see Lesser Treble-bar *opposite*). One feature that is visible to the naked eye is the changing direction of the cross-line nearest to the moth's head. The Lesser Treble-bar usually has a sharper kink in this line (near the edge of the wing) than does the Treble-bar. Both are common species. The Treble-bar can be found almost anywhere, particularly in hot, dry locations. It flies at dusk, but is frequently disturbed from rest during the day and can then easily be seen. There are two generations in the south but just one in the north. The eggs hatch in early autumn and the reddish-brown caterpillars hibernate during the winter, resuming feeding in the spring before crawling to the ground to pupate in early May.

Common throughout Britain and Ireland

Where found:	Almost anywhere, including gardens, heathland, moorland, field margins, sand dunes
When flying:	May–June and August–September in the south; July–August in the north
Forewing length:	19–22 mm
Larval foodplants:	St John's-worts

Similar species: Lesser Treble-bar

The first cross line is less kinked near the edge of the forewing compared to the Lesser Treble-bar

×4 **Lesser Treble-bar**   *Aplocera efformata* 1868

The Lesser Treble-bar is very similar to the Treble-bar except that it is slightly smaller and duller. Both species have two generations a year and fly at the same time, and their caterpillars feed on the same foodplants, St John's-worts. Although common, the Lesser Treble-bar is found mainly in the south of England and is rarer in Wales and farther north. In comparison, the Treble-bar is distributed throughout Britain and Ireland.

In addition to the slightly different kink in the first cross-line on their forewings (see Treble-bar *opposite*), these two similar moths can be distinguished if the tips of their abdomens can be seen. The tips are blunter (for both sexes) for this species than they are for the Treble-bar, which are more pointed. Because the difference between the two species is so small, perhaps it is not surprising that the Lesser Treble-bar was not recognized as a separate species until the 1920s and did not appear in Richard South's classic two-volume *Moths of the British Isles*, published in 1932. As a result, old records of the abundance of both species are unreliable.

Common in the south of England; local in Wales and northern England	
Where found:	Chalk grassland, woodland rides, gardens, cliff tops
When flying:	May–June and August–September
Forewing length:	16–19 mm
Larval foodplants:	St John's–worts
Similar species:	Treble-bar

The first cross line is more kinked near the edge of the forewing compared to the Treble-bar

×4 **Chimney Sweeper** *Odezia atrata* **1870**

Freshly emerged Chimney Sweepers have a white fringe around the tips of their upperwings, but otherwise they are entirely sooty-black, hence their name. There can sometimes be hundreds of adults perching together on tall grasses, where they make an impressive sight. Both sexes fly in sunshine and sometimes males will also fly in dull weather. This species may be seen on grassland or flying along hedgerows, usually in damp places, and are most common in the north. They are rapid movers, continually flying short distances, and as they never stay still for long are difficult to photograph.

Chimney Sweepers remain in the egg stage for a long period of time – from the end of summer, right through the winter, until the middle of the following spring. When the looping, green caterpillars hatch, they feed exclusively on the flowers and seeds of Pignut, and have only a few weeks to mature before pupating, doing so just below the ground surface at the end of May.

Common; well distributed in Britain but local in the south and south-east; frequent in the north; local in Ireland	
Where found:	Often found near streams and in damp, grassy places; more restricted in the south to sites on chalky or limestone soil
When flying:	June and July
Forewing length:	12–15 mm
Larval foodplant:	Pignut
Similar species: None	

×4 **Small White Wave** *Asthena albulata* 1875

This dainty little moth has several wavy yellowish-brown lines curving across its silky, white wings. It inhabits broad-leaved woodland, particularly ancient woodlands, where its caterpillars feed on the foliage of various deciduous trees. It flies mainly at the end of the day but, when disturbed, also flies readily in daylight.

There may be two generations in the south of England, but usually there is only one. The caterpillars are bluish-green with yellow-and-red markings. They are found on Hazel, Hornbeam, birches, wild roses, and probably other trees. By the end of August (later if there is a second generation), they are fully grown and descend to pupate on the ground under dead leaves or other litter. There they remain throughout the winter until the next generation emerges the following May.

Fairly common throughout the southern half of England and Wales, becoming scarcer and more local farther north through Scotland; scarce in Ireland

Where found:	Broad-leaved woodland
When flying:	May–early July and sometimes a partial second brood in August–mid-September
Forewing length:	9–11 mm
Larval foodplants:	Hazel, Hornbeam, birches, wild roses etc.

Similar species: None

×4 # Drab Looper

Minoa murinata　1878

The Drab Looper is, as its name suggests, a small, drab moth with pale-brown, unpatterned wings. Like all moths in the family Geometridae, its caterpillars are 'loopers' that move by curving their bodies into loops as they crawl over their foodplant. Why 'looper' is included in the English name for this species and Rannoch Looper (*page 111*) is unclear, since hundreds of other moths have caterpillars that are also 'loopers'. The Drab Looper is a relatively scarce species and found only in sunny woodland clearings south of the Wash, with areas that have been recently coppiced being particularly good places to look.

In sunny weather, males are on the wing in the middle of the day, and both sexes may be disturbed from low vegetation. Sometimes, they may be seen nectaring on low-growing flowers near their caterpillars' foodplant. Their dark, reddish-brown caterpillars feed on the flowers and floral leaves of Wood Spurge. Usually there is one generation a year, with an occasional partial second generation. It passes the winter as a pupa in a silken cocoon on the ground.

Nationally Scarce B
Legislative listing: NERC Act (S41 & S42)
UK BAP Priority Species
Scarce and local in southern England and the Welsh borders

Where found:	Sunny woodland clearings and rides
When flying:	May–June and sometimes August
Forewing length:	9–11 mm
Larval foodplant:	Wood Spurge
Similar species:	None

Latticed Heath

×4

At first you may think that this is a butterfly because it flies in sunshine, basks with its wings open and often settles with them raised up over its body. Almost all other moths fold their wings down along their bodies when at rest. The ground-colour is usually yellowish but varies, and in the Irish subspecies *hugginsi* is strikingly white. There is usually a lattice grid-pattern of brown markings on both the upperside and underside of the wings, but this can also vary.

Latticed Heaths are widely distributed over grassy heathland, moorland, gardens and waste ground. They may be seen throughout Britain and Ireland, although in Scotland usually only in the southern half.

The caterpillars have two colour forms, and may be either greenish or purplish, lined with white, and feed on Lucerne, clovers and trefoils. Fields of Lucerne (the animal forage plant also known as Alfalfa) can be a big attraction. Except in the north, there are two generations a year, and caterpillars can therefore be found at any time from early June to late September. They crawl under the loose surface of the ground to pupate and remain dormant there until emerging the following May.

Legislative listing: NERC Act (S41 & S42)

Priority Species (Northern Ireland)

UK BAP Priority Species (research)

Common and widely distributed in Britain and Ireland

Where found:	Open grassland including moors and waste ground, and heathland
When flying:	May–June and August–September
Forewing length:	11–15 mm
Larval foodplants:	Lucerne, clovers, trefoils

Similar species: Common Heath (*page 118*) and Netted Mountain Moth (*page 110*), although these do not raise their wings when at rest

×4 # Netted Mountain Moth   *Macaria carbonaria* 1895

This small, scarce, moth is only found in the central Scottish Highlands. On calm, sunny days, both sexes can be seen, sometimes in good numbers, fluttering over vegetation containing the caterpillars' food plant, Bearberry, a low-growing evergreen shrub. In windy weather (often the case in the Highlands) they behave very differently and only walk or make short flights from plant to plant. There is one generation a year, with moths on the wing early in the season, from April to early June.

The Netted Mountain Moth can be confused with the highly variable Common Heath (*page 118*) or Latticed Heath (*page 109*). Male Common Heaths can be distinguished by their strongly feathered antennae. Latticed Heaths have a crisper pattern and hold their wings like a small butterfly.

The dingy-brownish caterpillars feed at night from May to July on the young fresh shoots of Bearberry. They pupate in a cocoon among mosses and debris on the ground and spend the next eight months lying dormant before emerging late the following spring.

Nationally Rare
Scottish Biodiversity List
UK BAP Priority Species (ssp. *scotica*)
Scarce, restricted to the central highlands of Scotland

Where found:	Mountains and high moorland
When flying:	April–early June
Forewing length:	10–11 mm
Larval foodplant:	Bearberry

Similar species: Common Heath (*page 118*), Latticed Heath (*page 109*) and Black Mountain Moth (*page 122*) (different wing pattern)

× 4 # Rannoch Looper

Itame brunneata **1896**

The Rannoch Looper is a distinctive but very scarce and localized moth restricted to central Scotland. It inhabits mature birch or pine woodland and areas of scrub, but only where there is a good ground cover of Bilberry. Males fly back and forth over the Bilberry, usually in the afternoon, and both sexes are easily disturbed from their resting places, even on dull days.

They have one generation a year, with adults on the wing in mid-summer. As this does not leave much time for the immature stages to develop before bad weather sets in, eggs laid in July usually remain dormant throughout the winter before they hatch the following April. The twig-like caterpillars then feed rapidly on young Bilberry shoots and pupate in time for adult moths to emerge in June. It is thought that sometimes the pupal stage may extend for a full year, or more, but this has not been confirmed in the wild. As the moth's name implies, its caterpillars are loopers, as are all members of the family Geometridae (see *page 66*).

Nationally Scarce A	
Resident in central Scotland, but occasionally recorded in the lowlands of Scotland and parts of England, the result of immigration from continental Europe	
Where found:	Birch and pine woodland with Bilberry below
When flying:	Late June–July
Forewing length:	11–13 mm
Larval foodplants:	Bilberry, possibly also Cowberry

Similar species: None

A male (*inset*) in the usual resting position with wings closed like a butterfly and a female (*below*) showing the distinctive upperwing pattern

×4 **Little Thorn** *Cepphis advenaria* 1901

This scarce woodland moth only occurs in localized colonies, mainly in the south of England and southern Ireland. It can be an elusive species: for example, after being discovered first in East Sussex in 1851, it was thought to have been extinct there for many years before being rediscovered in the original wood in 2010.

The Little Thorn may occasionally be found on sunny days fluttering over low vegetation at the edges of woodland rides. This is one of the few species of day-flying moth that rests with its wings held above its body, like a butterfly, but not quite touching and tilted forward. A distinctive feature of this moth is that the rear edge of the hindwing has an obvious 'double-curve'.

There is one generation a year with adults flying from late May to the end of June. The greyish-brown caterpillars feed on the foliage of Bilberry. However, as this species is sometimes found at sites where there is no Bilberry, the caterpillars probably feed on other plants, possibly including Bramble. They pupate for the winter in late August.

Nationally Scarce B
Small colonies occur throughout the south of England and in southern Ireland

Where found:	Open woodland edges, rides and scrub, often on heavy damp soils
When flying:	May–June
Forewing length:	14–17 mm
Larval foodplant:	Bilberry

Similar species: The sandy-brown coloured Dingy Shell *Euchoeca nebulata* is a woodland species that also settles like a butterfly. It flies from dusk but may be disturbed near its foodplant, Alder, during the day. It is smaller (FL: 9–12 mm).

×4 **Brown Silver-line** *Petrophora chlorosata* 1902

The Brown Silver-line usually flies at dusk and at night. However, it can often be seen during the day, sometimes in numbers, if it is disturbed by walking through Bracken. It can be found wherever Bracken grows and is fairly common over the whole of Britain and Ireland except for the Scottish Highlands. Its forewings, which are usually pinkish-brown, have two brown cross-lines edged with white, and there is a small, dark spot between the two lines.

The caterpillars may be olive-green or reddish-brown and can be found feeding on Bracken from mid-June to early September. Like caterpillars of all the family Geometridae, they are 'loopers'. There are three pairs of fully functional legs at the front, but only two pairs of claspers or prolegs at the back. When resting, they have the habit of grasping a twig by their back legs and suspending their body so that it pokes out like a dead twig. In the autumn, they crawl down to pupate just under the ground surface.

Common throughout Britain and Ireland, except for the Highlands of Scotland	
Where found:	Heathland, moorland and woodlands with Bracken
When flying:	Mid-April–June
Forewing length:	15–18 mm
Larval foodplant:	Bracken
Similar species: None	

× 4 # Dark Bordered Beauty

Epione vespertaria **1908**

This rare and very local species occurs in only a few sites in Scotland and one in northern England. It is similar to the commoner Bordered Beauty *Epione repandaria*, but that species is not usually seen during the day. At some sites, male Dark Bordered Beauties often fly habitually during the day and both sexes are easily disturbed from the larval foodplants. Males are darker than females and their dark border is of a constant width (rather than tapering towards the forewing tip as in the Bordered Beauty). Females are lemon yellow and their reddish-brown border varies in width.

There is one generation a year, with adults flying at the end of summer. Eggs laid in August overwinter until the following April before hatching. The greyish-brown caterpillars feed in May and June and pupate in time for the next generation of adults to be on the wing in July (occasionally late June). In Scotland, the foodplant is young Aspen (less than 50 cm high); in England it is Creeping Willow (a very low-growing shrub) and possibly other willows.

Nationally Rare	
Legislative listing: NERC Act (S41)	
UK BAP Priority Species	
Rare and local; only a few sites in Scotland and one in the Vale of York	

Where found:	Damp heathland and open woodland
When flying:	July–August
Forewing length:	12–14 mm
Larval foodplants:	Low Aspen scrub, Creeping Willow, possibly other species of willow

Similar species: Bordered Beauty *Epione repandaria* (but this is not normally seen during the day)

Male

×4 **Speckled Yellow** *Pseudopanthera macularia* 1909

This very distinctive moth flies in sunny weather and, although locally distributed, is often seen in numbers. It favours open woodland and scrub, and although it may be found widely over Britain and southern Ireland, there are only scattered records from many areas.

There is one generation a year, with moths on the wing from mid-May to the end of June. The caterpillars, which are green, lined with white, are usually found on Wood Sage, although White Dead-nettle, woundworts and Yellow Archangel may also be used. By the end of August, they have climbed down to the ground before pupating on or just below the surface under dead leaves and other plant debris. They remain here throughout the winter before the next generation emerges the following spring.

Locally common in the south of England, Wales and Ireland; more local farther north	
Where found:	Open woodland, and scrubby grassland
When flying:	Mid-May–June
Forewing length:	13–15mm
Larval foodplants:	Wood Sage, woundworts, White Dead–nettle, Yellow Archangel
Similar species: None	

× 4 # Belted Beauty

Lycia zonaria **1928**

This very scarce moth can be found at only a few coastal sites in western Britain and in Ireland. The preferred habitat is low-lying coastal plains (called machair in Scotland and Ireland), vegetated sand dunes and, sometimes, sandy saltings.

Males may be seen flying in afternoon sunshine or sitting on vegetation, but females are wingless and unable to fly. A distinguishing feature (of both sexes) is the series of closely spaced orange rings (or 'belts') that encircle their abdomen. The Rannoch Brindled Beauty looks superficially similar, but instead of the orange 'belts', has a line of orange spots along the top of its abdomen. However, there should be no real scope for confusion as the two species occur in very different habitats.

Adults fly early in the year and females have been seen laying their eggs in cracks in wooden posts, a habit shared with the Rannoch Brindled Beauty. The caterpillars, which are greenish with two yellow-and-black stripes, may be found on Common Bird's-foot-trefoil, Kidney Vetch and other low plants from May to July. They pupate just below ground in August, ready for the long wait until the following March.

Nationally Rare	
Legislative listing: NERC Act (S41 & S42)	
UK BAP Priority Species	
Rare and local in north Wales and north-west England, western Scotland and in Ireland	
Where found:	Machair, grassy sand dunes and rarely on saltings
When flying:	March and April
Forewing length:	13–16 mm (male); female wingless
Larval foodplants:	Common Bird's-foot-trefoil, Kidney Vetch, clovers, etc.

Similar species: Rannoch Brindled Beauty

Male

Female

× 4 **Rannoch Brindled Beauty** *Lycia lapponaria* **1929**

The Rannoch Brindled Beauty is regarded as one of our scarcest moths and the high moorlands of central and northern Scotland are its principal habitat. However, it is possibly under-recorded and may be more widespread. The males' greyish wings are semi-transparent with distinct black veins, whereas the females are wingless. Both sexes have a prominent line of orange spots on their abdomens.

Although males rarely fly during the day, they are often seen because they have the curious habit of resting in the open on posts and lichen-covered fences. Females also behave in this way, and sometimes there will be several males and females on the same post. The eggs are sometimes laid directly onto the posts and the infant caterpillars then have to crawl down to their foodplant nearby. They feed mainly on Bog-myrtle or Bilberry, from mid-May to early August, before pupating underground. When fully grown, the caterpillars are reddish-brown with black-and-yellow markings. There is evidence that the pupae may remain dormant for several years, but more research is needed on this intriguing moth.

Nationally Scarce A	
Rare, in central and northern Scotland	
Where found:	Moorland
When flying:	Late March–early May
Forewing length:	14–16 mm (male); female wingless
Larval foodplants:	Bog-myrtle, Bilberry, heathers, etc.

Similar species: Belted Beauty, but that species favours coastal sites

Male

Female

117

×4 **Common Heath**   *Ematurga atomaria*   1952

The Common Heath is indeed common throughout Britain and Ireland. Although predominantly found on heathland, it also occurs in meadows, woodland rides and on calcareous grassland. On heathland and moorland, its caterpillars feed on heathers, but elsewhere they feed on clovers, vetches and trefoils. This is a variable species whose ground-colour can range from almost white (for females) through dusky-yellow to dark-grey. Both forewing and hindwing have several dark brown bands of variable width, sometimes merging together, sometimes blurred or freckled. The Latticed Heath (*page 109*) is similar, although usually has better-defined markings. Common Heaths rest with their wings held flat, whereas Latticed Heaths usually hold their wings closed over their backs like a butterfly. The male Common Heath (illustrated) has very feathery antennae, which distinguishes it from the Netted Mountain Moth (restricted to the Scottish Highlands – *page 110*) and similar-looking butterflies, such as the Dingy Skipper and Grizzled Skipper. On northern moorlands there is a smaller form f. *minuta*.

Usually there is only one generation, but there may be a partial second generation, especially in southern Britain, and adults can therefore be seen on the wing in May-June and again in August. The caterpillars, which may be any shade of greenish/brown, purple or grey with white markings, may be found feeding from mid-June to the start of autumn.

Common and widespread	
Where found:	Heathland, moorland, open woodland, meadows, verges
When flying:	May–June and sometimes August
Forewing length:	12–15 mm
Larval foodplants:	Heather, Bell Heather, Cross-leaved Heath, clovers, trefoils, vetches

Similar species: Latticed Heath (*page 109*), Netted Mountain Moth (*page 110*) (smaller)

118

×4 # Bordered White

Bupalus piniaria **1954**

The Bordered White is quite common throughout Britain and Ireland, particularly where there is Scots Pine or plantations of other coniferous trees. On warm days they may be seen fluttering around conifers, or can be disturbed by shaking their branches. Bordered Whites are on the wing in early summer in the south, though rather later in the north. When at rest, this species holds its wings together above its body, like a butterfly. There are substantial differences between males and females, as well as regional variations. The upperside of the wings of females are more orangey-yellow and have less patterning than those of males. Moths of both sexes found in the north tend to have brighter colours than those in the south.

The long, thin caterpillars are greenish with whitish-yellow markings. They feed on the young needles of conifers and occasionally can become a pest in plantations. In early autumn, they crawl down to the ground and pupate on or just below the ground under a covering of conifer needles.

Common throughout Britain and Ireland	
Where found:	Coniferous woodland and plantations
When flying:	May–June in the south, continuing as late as early August in the north
Forewing length:	16–18 mm
Larval foodplants:	Scots Pine and many other conifers
Similar species: None	

Male

Female

× 4 # Scotch Annulet

Gnophos obfuscatus 1963

Although the Scotch Annulet looks very similar to its widespread and close relative the Annulet, it is restricted to rocky mountains and moorlands in Scotland and Ireland. The Annulet favours coastal sites. Both species have a ground-colour that is variable, from light-grey to dark-brown, and a similar delicate pattern of freckled bands. However, the Scotch Annulet is slightly bigger, and the 'annulets' (or small rings) in the middle of each wing tend not be hollow, as in the Annulet, or so distinct.

Like the Annulet, it may be seen during the day in July and August resting in the open on rocks and stones, but as it is so well camouflaged you may have to look carefully to find it. It is also easily disturbed. The life-cycles of the Scotch Annulet and Annulet are similar. The rather stout, greyish caterpillars overwinter on the ground and pupate the following spring in a cocoon under plant debris. The two species generally feed on different foodplants, with the Scotch Annulet favouring heathers and other moorland plants. However, as Annulet caterpillars have sometimes been reported to occur on Heather, the two species can be confused.

Nationally Scarce B	
Only found locally in the north and west of Scotland and in western Ireland	
Where found:	Rocky moorland, gullies etc.
When flying:	July–August
Forewing length:	17–21 mm
Larval foodplants:	Heather, Bell Heather, Cross-leaved Heath, Petty Whin, saxifrages, stonecrops and probably other plants

Similar species: Annulet (slightly smaller), Black Mountain Moth (*page 122*) (much smaller)

×4 **Annulet** *Charissa obscurata* 1964

The Annulet is a widespread and highly variable species, with populations that live on chalk downland tending to be lighter (some being almost white) than those that inhabit areas with dark rocks or peaty soils. The pattern of the markings tends to remain the same in all colour forms, and it has (usually) a hollow ring (or annulet) in the middle of each wing, but the markings can be difficult to see in dark individuals. Annulets do not habitually fly during the day but are readily disturbed from their resting place. They tend to settle on exposed rocks and stones where they merge into their surroundings, but, with practice (and a bit of luck!), can be found. They are most frequently encountered during July and August at rocky coastal locations around the south-west of England and Wales and the western coasts of Scotland and Ireland.

The rather dumpy, predominantly grey/brown caterpillars feed on a wide range of low-growing plants. There are two other very similar species. The Scotch Annulet is slightly larger than the Annulet but its rings (or annulets) are not usually so distinct and it favours the Scottish moors rather than coastal locations. The rare Irish Annulet *Odontognophos dumetata* looks very similar but is found only in the Burren area of County Clare in Ireland, and is not usually a day-flier.

Fairly common on suitable habitat; possibly declining	
Where found:	Rocky coasts and cliffs around south-west England, Wales, western Scotland and Ireland; dry heathland and occasionally chalk downland, mainly in southern England
When flying:	July–August
Forewing length:	15–18 mm
Larval foodplants:	Sea Campion, Thrift, Common Rock-rose, Thyme, Heather, etc.

Similar species: Scotch Annulet, Irish Annulet *Odontognophos dumetata* (very similar, but not normally day-flying)

× 4 # Black Mountain Moth   *Glacies coracina* `1965`

As its name suggests, the Black Mountain Moth can only be found on mountains, generally above about 600 m (2,000 ft), in central and northern Scotland. Its very rounded wings give it a rather unusual appearance. Females are slightly smaller than males and not as dark. Both sexes are often seen crawling on the ground or on vegetation and males are only seen flying on warm, still days at the height of summer. Their dark colour absorbs radiation from the sun and helps to keep them warm.

The Black Mountain Moth is not particularly well known, but it probably has a two-year life-cycle, since the population appears to peak every other year. The caterpillars grow very slowly and may take two years to reach maturity, surviving through two winters. They feed on Crowberry, a dwarf evergreen shrub, and pupate in late spring under moss or plant debris.

This species in unlikely to be confused with any other moth but can occur in the same locations as the Netted Mountain Moth (*page 110*) (slightly smaller and feeding on Bearberry) and Scotch Annulet (*page 120*) (larger and feeding on a range of moorland plants).

Nationally Rare	
Widespread but local in central and northern Scotland	
Where found:	Highlands of Scotland above 600 m
When flying:	June–July
Forewing length:	10–13 mm
Larval foodplant:	Crowberry

Similar species: Netted Mountain Moth (*page 110*) (smaller), Scotch Annulet (*page 120*) (larger) occur in the same habitat

Black-veined Moth

×4

Siona lineata 1966

This very distinctive moth has always been confined to the south of England but is now restricted to just a few sites on chalk downland in Kent. The grass sward must be long with plentiful Wild Marjoram, Common Knapweed and Common Bird's-foot-trefoil, all of which are foodplants for its caterpillars. June is the best month to find the adult moths, which fly during the day if the weather is good, as well as at dusk. They take nectar from flowers, including Common Bird's-foot-trefoil and Bramble. Often they hold their wings closed or partly closed, like a butterfly.

Males have a long, thin body. Females are smaller, with stouter, shorter bodies and shorter wings. The Black-veined Moth is unlikely to be confused with any other moth. However, the Sulphur Pearl *Sitochroa palealis* (see *page 195*), which is a large micro-moth that can be active by day, also occurs in rough grassland and has a similar underwing pattern – but it is a different shape and never rests with its wings held up. The long, thin caterpillars are grey/brown with darker lines. They overwinter before pupating in a cocoon attached to a plant stem.

LEGALLY PROTECTED: W&C Act (Sched. 5)

British Red Data Book (Endangered)

Legislative listing: NERC Act (S41)

UK BAP Priority Species

Very rare, now restricted to a few sites in Kent

Where found:	Chalk downland
When flying:	Late May–early July
Forewing length:	19–22 mm
Larval foodplants:	Wild Marjoram, Common Knapweed, Common Bird's-foot-trefoil, possibly others

Similar species: Sulphur Pearl *Sitochroa palealis* (see *page 195*)

Confusion with the Black-veined White butterfly may have been possible in the past, but that species is now extinct in Britain.

× 4 # Straw Belle

Aspitates gilvaria 1967

The Straw Belle and Yellow Belle are about the same size and very similar in appearance. Both are easily disturbed when resting in low vegetation. Straw Belle has one generation a year and frequents tussocky chalk grassland and old chalk quarries. In contrast, Yellow Belle has two generations and is usually found near the coast on sand dunes, saltmarshes, and vegetated shingle. Both species pass the winter as a small caterpillar. The Straw Belle, the rarer of the two species, may be found only on the North Downs of southern England and in the Burren region of western Ireland, where the separate subspecies *burrenensis* is darker and has a longer hindwing stripe.

Caterpillars are predominantly yellowish-grey with dark lines along their back and sides. The eggs hatch in September and caterpillars hibernate when small, resuming feeding in the spring on a range of low-growing wild flowers. They pupate in a flimsy cocoon in the grass in time for adults to emerge from mid-June to early July. For some reason, emergence is usually found to be slightly earlier in Kent than it is in Surrey.

Legislative listing: NERC Act (S41)

UK BAP Priority Species

Rare in south-east England and locally fairly common in the Burren region of Ireland

Where found:	Chalk and limestone grassland, including quarries
When flying:	Mid-June or July–August
Forewing length:	15–18 mm
Larval foodplants:	Common Bird's-foot-trefoil, Fairy Flax, Creeping Cinquefoil, Thyme, etc.

Similar species: Yellow Belle

×4 · # Yellow Belle

Semiaspitates ochrearia 1968

The Yellow Belle is predominantly found around the coasts of southern England and Wales, where it favours sand dunes, vegetated shingle and saltmarshes. It may also be found on grassland and heathland at a few inland sites, but these are the exception. This species usually flies from dusk but is readily disturbed from rest during the day, and often flies freely during the day in hot summer weather. Although the it is normally slightly smaller than the Straw Belle, the sizes do overlap, but the Yellow Belle can be distinguished by its deeper yellow colour and two (rather than one) forewing stripes, although sometimes these stripes can be quite faint. Females are usually less yellow than males and they do not have feathery antennae.

There are two generations with a few weeks between them. The caterpillars feed on a wide range of herbaceous plants, and are yellowish-brown, lined with darker brown. The winter generation hibernates before resuming feeding in the spring.

Locally common around the coast of southern England and Wales; also found at a few inland heaths, including the brecklands of Norfolk and Suffolk

Where found:	Coastal grassland, sand dunes, vegetated shingle, waste ground
When flying:	May–June and August–September
Forewing length:	12–17 mm
Larval foodplants:	A wide range of species including Wild Carrot, Buck's-horn Plantain, Sea Wormwood, Common Bird's-foot-trefoil

Similar species: Straw Belle

× 4 **Grey Scalloped Bar** *Dyscia fagaria* **1969**

The Grey Scalloped Bar is a distinctive, medium-sized moth that inhabits open moorland, heathland and boggy ground with a preference for areas with short vegetation. Males like to rest on stones or bare ground and are easily disturbed. They are larger than females and lighter in colour. Populations on upland habitats are usually lighter than those that occur on lowland heaths. During the day, males may be quite active but females do not usually fly until after dusk, when both sexes are on the wing together. Their distribution is patchy, and you are more likely to see this species in northern localities than in southern areas.

The caterpillars are pinkish-brown, with white and grey markings. They grow slowly at first, hibernating during the winter, and resuming feeding in the spring. Then they can be found after dark, feeding on fresh shoots of various heathers. In May, they pupate in a cocoon attached to the foodplant, or in leaf-litter on the ground.

Locally common in suitable habitat, but scarce across most of southern England	
Where found:	Moorland, heathland and boggy ground
When flying:	June–July
Forewing length:	15–21 mm
Larval foodplants:	Heather, Bell Heather and Cross-leaved Heath

Similar species: None

×4 **Grass Wave** *Perconia strigillaria* 1970

The Grass Wave, Common Wave *Cabera exanthemata* and Common White Wave *C. pusaria* are medium-sized moths that are similar in appearance. However, although all three may be disturbed from rest, only the Grass Wave regularly flies during the day. It can be distinguished by its light-grey background and dark stripes; the other two species being much paler. It is also typically slightly larger and has less rounded wings.

Grass Waves can be encountered frequently on heathland in the south of England, particularly the lowland heaths of Surrey. They can also be found in dry, open woodland and on moorland and boggy heathland elsewhere across Britain and Ireland, but here populations tend to be patchily distributed.

The purplish-grey caterpillars feed on heathers, Broom and Petty Whin and have also been reported on Blackthorn and eating the flowers of Gorse. They hibernate during the winter, reaching full-size in May, when they pupate in a cocoon attached to their foodplant.

Widespread; locally common in southern England but generally scarce elsewhere	
Where found:	Heathland, open woodland, moorland
When flying:	May–July
Forewing length:	15–20 mm
Larval foodplants:	Heather, Bell Heather, Broom, Petty Whin, and possibly Blackthorn and Gorse

Similar species: Common Wave *Cabera exanthemata*, Common White Wave *C. pusaria* (not usually day-flyers)

Hawk-moths
Family: Sphingidae

11 regularly occurring British species
3 day-flying

Hawk-moths are among our most impressive moths. There are over 1,000 different hawk-moth species in the world but only eleven of them are recorded regularly in Britain and Ireland. Of these, three are day-flyers.

The most frequently and widely encountered day-flyer is the intriguing Hummingbird Hawk-moth. Because it is an immigrant and the number that arrive in the British Isles depends largely on weather conditions in continental Europe, it can be fairly common in some years but very rare in others. At any time during sunny summer weather, a Hummingbird Hawk-moth may be seen hovering in front of a flower, its long tongue delving deep to drink the nectar. However, photographing this species is a huge challenge since the moth's wings never stop as it jinks suddenly from flower to flower, staying in one place for only a few seconds.

Although, in recent years, Hummingbird Hawk-moths have bred and survived the winter in south-west England, the vast majority that are seen in Britain and Ireland are newly arrived immigrants. In contrast, the other two day-flying hawk-moths, the Broad-bordered and Narrow-bordered Bee Hawk-moths, are resident breeding species. They are very similar in appearance and behaviour, resemble bumblebees and usually feed on the wing, hovering like Hummingbird Hawk-moths. The Broad-bordered Bee Hawk-moth is restricted to the southern half of England and Wales. The Narrow-bordered Bee Hawk-moth, which has declined in recent years, is now spread thinly over south-west England, south Wales and Scotland, and in Ireland, where the Burren is a reliable site. Both species occur in East Anglia: Broad-bordered in the Brecklands and Narrow-bordered in Thetford Forest on the Norfolk/Suffolk border, where it is now only seen occasionally.

Sometimes, one of the night-flying hawk-moths may be found resting by day, perhaps on a fencepost or in an open conservatory. The Lime *Mimas tiliae*, Privet *Sphinx ligustri*, Poplar *Laothoe populi* and Eyed *Smerinthus ocellata* Hawk-moths may all be discovered in this way. Most of the other night-flyers are rarer and less likely to be seen. These four rely entirely on the store of food that they have accumulated as caterpillars as they do not have a functioning proboscis and so cannot feed as adults. In contrast, the Elephant Hawk-moth *Deilephila elpenor* and its relative the Small Elephant Hawk-moth *D. porcellus* do drink nectar and, very occasionally, may also may be found by day, perhaps resting on honeysuckle. As well as being a source of nectar, this also provides good camouflage for their beautiful pink-and-brown colours.

Poplar Hawk-moth
Laothoe populi
(FL: 30–46 mm)

Examples of night-flying hawk-moths that may be encountered during the day

Lime Hawk-moth
Mimas tiliae
(FL: 24–38 mm)

f. *brunnea*

Small Elephant Hawk-moth
Deilephila porcellus
(FL: 21–24 mm)

Elephant Hawk-moth ▶
Deilephila elpenor
(FL: 27–33 mm)

Further examples of night-flying hawk-moths that may be encountered during the day

Eyed Hawk-moth
Smerinthus ocellata
(FL: 36–44 mm)

Privet Hawk-moth
Sphinx ligustri
(FL: 41–55 mm)

×3 **Hummingbird Hawk-moth**   *Macroglossum stellatarum* 1984

There is a legend that Hummingbird Hawk-moths are messengers of good tidings. They are immigrants from southern Europe and northern Africa, which, in a good year, can occur throughout Britain and Ireland. This migratory habit is the main reason that numbers can vary so much from year to year, as the species' fortunes depend upon what happens at its main breeding sites, and on the prevailing weather conditions right across Europe. Occasionally, adult moths have been found hibernating in parts of south-west Britain, and the species may possibly be established and breeding here, though perhaps only temporarily. Usually, only one individual is seen at a time, moving rapidly between flowers and stopping for just a few seconds to hover, like a hummingbird, with its long tongue reaching for nectar, before hurrying on to the next flower. Mostly, they fly when it is sunny but they are also sometimes seen in overcast conditions.

Frequent immigrant: common in some years, rare in others	
Where found:	Anywhere, but most often in the south and near the coast
When flying:	In sunshine throughout the summer and autumn; occasionally at other times of year
Forewing length:	19–24 mm
Larval foodplants:	Lady's Bedstraw, Hedge Bedstraw, Wild Madder
Similar species: None	

Although there are two broods a year in the Mediterranean, there is only one in more northern latitudes. The caterpillars may be found from June to October. They vary in colour, having different shades of yellowish-green, with prominent white lines, and the 'horn', a characteristic feature of all hawk-moth caterpillars, is bluish with a yellowish-brown tip. They pupate in a loose cocoon on or close to the ground under their foodplant.

× 3   **Narrow-bordered Bee Hawk-moth**   *Hemaris tityus*   1982

Although the bee hawk-moths resemble large bumblebees, they are much quicker and more agile in flight, and more easily disturbed if approached. The Narrow-bordered Bee Hawk-moth is slightly smaller than its near-relative, the Broad-bordered Bee Hawk-moth, and, as the name suggests, its mostly transparent wings have a narrower dark border. Occasionally, freshly emerged adults may be encountered. At this stage their wings have a dusky-grey covering of scales but this rapidly wears off. They feed while hovering in front of 'long-trumpet' flowers such as Bugle, louseworts, Red Valerian and rhododendrons, moving rapidly from flower to flower. Usually they occur in damp pastures or on calcareous grassland, provided there are plenty of flowers to provide a good source of nectar. However, they may occasionally be found flying along woodland rides and on heathlands (habitats also favoured by the Broad-bordered Bee Hawk-moth).

There is one generation, which is on the wing early in the summer. The colourful caterpillars are green with variable yellow and reddish-brown markings, and can sometimes be located by the distinctive holes that they chew in scabious leaves during July. Like most hawk-moth caterpillars, they have a characteristic tail, which for this species is a finely pointed reddish-brown 'horn'. They pupate in a loose cocoon on the ground in August and remain there until the next generation emerges nine months later.

Nationally Scarce B	
Legislative listing: NERC Act (S41 & S42)	
Scottish Biodiversity List	
Priority Species (Northern Ireland)	
UK BAP Priority Species	

Scarce and local throughout much of Britain, but now extremely local or absent in south-eastern, eastern and much of northern England

Where found:	Damp grassland, calcareous grassland, occasionally woodland rides and heathland
When flying:	Late April–early July
Forewing length:	18–21 mm
Larval foodplants:	Devil's bit Scabious, occasionally Small and Field Scabiouses

Similar species: Broad-bordered Bee Hawk-moth

×3 **Broad-bordered Bee Hawk-moth** *Hemaris fuciformis* 1983

The Broad-bordered Bee Hawk-moth is very similar to the Narrow-bordered Bee Hawk-moth, and as the two can sometimes occur together in woodland rides or on heathland, a careful look is needed to determine the distinguishing features. In this species, the wings have a wider dark border and there is a dark bar part-way along the leading edge of the forewings. The colour of these features is usually reddish-brown, as are the bands on the abdomen. Like the Narrow-bordered Bee Hawk-moth, it feeds by hovering in front of flowers with a long 'trumpet', using its long tongue to reach in and suck up nectar. You are most likely to see this species in the middle of the day feeding on honeysuckles, although rhododendrons are another favourite and many other species of plant may be used.

The striking green caterpillars have red-and-yellow markings and a reddish-brown horn. As their favoured foodplant is Wild Honeysuckle, they are generally found in wooded or partially wooded locations, or on heathlands. Otherwise, the life-cycles of Broad-bordered Bee Hawk-moth and Narrow-bordered Bee Hawk-moth are similar. The caterpillars crawl down to the ground in late summer to hibernate in a silken cocoon just below the surface.

Nationally Scarce B	
Only occurs very locally in southern Britain north to Yorkshire, with strongholds in East Anglia, Lincolnshire and some woodlands in southern England	
Where found:	Open woodlands and clearings, lightly wooded heathland
When flying:	May–early July, with, occasionally, a second brood in August–September
Forewing length:	19–23 mm
Larval foodplants:	Wild Honeysuckle, occasionally cultivated varieties and Snowberry

Similar species: Narrow-bordered Bee Hawk–moth

133

Tussocks, Footmen, Tigers and Ermines
Family: Lymantriidae and Arctiidae

42 British species
12 day-flying

The mixed group of moths in this section comprise two families: the tussocks (family Lymantriidae); and the footmen, tigers and ermines (family Arctiidae).

The tussocks are a family of 'furry' moths, males of which have strongly feathered antennae. There are eleven species in Britain and Ireland, of which three fly during the day. They take their name from the characteristic tufts of hair on the backs of their ornate caterpillars. The most widely distributed species is the Vapourer, the males of which are often seen fluttering around trees and shrubs late in the season, usually well into October. It is only the males of both the Vapourer and Scarce Vapourer that fly. The females have only vestigial wings and are flightless, remaining close to the cocoon from which they emerged, in wait for a male to find them. The eggs are laid on the cocoon and remain there throughout the winter before hatching in the spring. The only other day-flying tussock is the Gypsy Moth and although the females can fly, it seems that they, too, never stray far from their cocoon.

Footmen usually hold their long, narrow wings folded tightly against their slim bodies. Two species are day-fliers: the Red-necked Footman and the Dew Moth. The footman flies high in coniferous forests though frequently descends to ground level. The Dew Moth has a shape more characteristic of a noctuid (see *page 148*). Caterpillars of both species are hairy and feed on lichens and algae.

The day-flying tigers are relatively common and easy to find in certain parts of Britain and Ireland. The most widely distributed is the Ruby Tiger, which flies by day and by night. There are two generations in the south, the first of which is more likely to be seen during the day, early in the year. There are several other colourful day-flying tigers, the Wood Tiger, Jersey Tiger and Scarlet Tiger, all of which are unmistakable given a good view. The Garden Tiger *Arctia caja*, although not a day-flyer, has caterpillars that are seen frequently as they are so conspicuous when fully grown. They are often referred to as 'woolly bears' and may be found almost anywhere feeding on low plants, very often near the coast.

Ermine moths are in the same family and sub-family as tigers (family Arctiidae, sub-family Arctiinae) and one, the Muslin Moth, is a day-flyer. Ermines are less colourful than the tigers but have attractive light-coloured wings that are spotted with black. They are referred to as 'ermines' because they reminded early entomologists of the ermine robes worn by members of the peerage.

Although different in many ways, the Cinnabar is included within the family Arctiidae. It is one of our most easily recognized moths, flying during the day in many open habitats and sometimes in gardens. Its conspicuous and distinctive orange-and-black caterpillars feed openly, usually on Common Ragwort.

Male Vapourer

Ruby Tiger

Cinnabar

Red-necked Footman – a woodland species

Cinnabar caterpillars on Common Ragwort

'Woolly bear' caterpillar of **Garden Tiger**
Arctia caja on Common Ragwort

Murlough NNR, Co Antrim –
Wood Tiger habitat with not
a wood in sight!

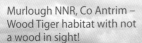

Wood Tiger

×4 # Scarce Vapourer

Orgyia recens **2025**

Although records indicate that the Scarce Vapourer was once widespread (but localized) in parts of England and Wales, it is now confined to just a few sites in Lincolnshire, south Yorkshire and Norfolk. Male Scarce Vapourers are slightly bigger and darker than its much commoner close relative the Vapourer, and have distinctive white markings near the tip of the forewings that the Vapourer lacks. They have a fluttering, unsteady flight as they search for females. The furry females are unable to fly as their 'wings' are just tiny stumps and instead wait for a mate near the cocoon that covers the remains of their pupal casing.

Scarce Vapourer caterpillars are black with mainly white and brown markings and with four pronounced tufts (or tussocks – hence the family name) of brown hairs standing up on the middle of their back. They also have a curious feature (in common with Vapourer caterpillars) in the long, thin tufts of black hairs that point out from their front and back ends. The purpose of these adornments is a mystery. They feed on a variety of woody shrubs and trees, and their cocoons are attached to their chosen foodplant. There is one main generation early in the summer, with a partial second generation later during the season.

British Red Data Book (Vulnerable)	
Legislative listing: NERC Act (S41)	
UK BAP Priority Species	
Rare and local, possibly overlooked	

Where found:	Lightly wooded fens, hedgerows, lowland heathland, coastal sand dunes
When flying:	June–July, and sometimes August–October if there is a second generation
Forewing length:	14–18 mm (male)
Larval foodplants:	Various broad-leaved trees and shrubs, including sallows, birches, Hawthorn and oaks

Similar species: Vapourer, which is much commoner

Female

Male

×4 **Vapourer** *Orgyia antiqua* `2026`

The Vapourer is a medium-sized moth that is widespread and common throughout much of Britain and Ireland. Although similar to the Scarce Vapourer, with the same fluttering flight, males are much plainer and have just one conspicuous white spot on each forewing. The females, which are unable to fly as they have only rudimentary stumps instead of wings, remain close to their pupa. They are not quite as furry as Scarce Vapourer females but are otherwise very similar. The female lays her eggs close to where she emerged, usually on the outside of her own cocoon. The eggs remain there throughout the winter, and the caterpillars emerge during the following May.

The caterpillars, which are grey and black with red spots, have four tussocks of yellowish-brown hairs standing up on the middle of their backs. Why they have this strange feature is unknown. Dispersal of this species depends on the caterpillars crawling to a new location, although they may take advantage of the wind to aid this process by swinging on a silken thread. They pupate in a cocoon attached to a twig or leaf or perhaps a nearby fence or other man-made structure. Adult moths are usually on the wing from July to October in the south, and from September to October farther north.

Common, locally throughout Britain and Ireland	
Where found:	Open woodland, hedges, moors, heathland, scrubby places, urban areas
When flying:	July–October
Forewing length:	12–17 mm (male)
Larval foodplants:	Many broad-leaved trees and shrubs, for example birches, Hazel, willows, elms, Blackthorn as well as cultivated shrubs like *Cotoneaster* and *Pyracantha*

Similar species: Scarce Vapourer

Female

Male

Gypsy Moth

×4

Lymantria dispar **2034**

Male and female Gypsy Moths look quite different. Males are brown with irregular, narrow, transverse bars and feathery antennae, and they can fly long distances in daylight. The much larger females are creamy-white and rarely fly very far from their cocoon. This species overwinters as eggs that are laid in large batches on the bark or leaves of a wide range of trees and shrubs. The eggs are covered in yellowish-brown hairs and scales from the abdomen of the female. The caterpillars hatch in April and are black with yellowish markings and have a double-row of spots along their back, some red, some blue. While still small, they disperse by 'ballooning' on the wind, hanging onto silk threads. As they mature, they can be identified by their blue spots (on the front segments of their bodies) and red spots (on the rear segments). They feed for up to three months before pupating in late June.

The Gypsy Moth was once common in parts of East Anglia, but became extinct as a breeding species by the early 1900s due to drainage of its breeding habitat. Until recently, it was only recorded occasionally as an immigrant, and only males were seen. However, there are now small breeding colonies in parts of London and in Buckinghamshire, and at one site on the Dorset/Hampshire border, all of which are thought to have become established from eggs imported accidentally. In mainland Europe and North America, the caterpillar of this species can completely defoliate plantations of trees, and this ability has led to it being classed as a potential pest; any sightings should be reported to the Forestry Commission (**www.forestry.gov.uk**).

British Red Data Book (Extinct)	
Rare immigrant. A few breeding colonies are known, probably derived from accidental introductions of eggs. Found regularly in the Channel Islands	
Where found:	Formerly in the fenland of East Anglia but now woodland, scrub and gardens
When flying:	July–September
Forewing length:	16–24 mm (male) 22–35 mm (female)
Larval foodplants:	Foliage of many broad–leaved trees

Similar species: Black Arches *Lymantria monacha* (smaller and not a day-flyer, but occasionally found at rest during the day)

Male

×4 **Dew Moth** *Setina irrorella* `2036`

Males of this distinctive, medium-sized moth fly in the early morning and then from late afternoon onwards. Both sexes rest in the open, hanging onto stems of grasses. The ground-colour of their forewings varies from yellowish-buff to creamy-white and they have three irregular rows of conspicuous small, dark spots. Females are slightly smaller than males.

The Dew Moth is rare and very local. It is mainly a coastal species, scattered around the south and west coasts, extending right up to the Hebrides, although it is occasionally also found inland. The Burren in County Clare in Ireland is a reliable site, but it has been found on the North Downs in Surrey and other places in the recent past.

The hairy caterpillars feed on lichens growing in grassland and on rocks and shingle in open areas, and are often seen in sunshine during the day. They are blackish-brown and grey, and have a broken line of yellow markings along their backs, and black hairs. Dew Moths pass the winter as caterpillars, pupating in a cocoon on the ground in May.

Nationally Scarce A	
Scarce and local mainly around the coast	
Where found:	Usually rocky or shingly coastal sites in the south and west; sometimes inland on chalk grassland and limestone pavement
When flying:	Late May–July
Forewing length:	11–18 mm; female slightly smaller than male
Larval foodplants:	Lichens
Similar species: None	

× 4 # Red-necked Footman *Atolmis rubricollis* `2039`

This is an unmistakable moth with velvety black wings and a red collar. Its abdomen is partly black and partly orange. It is the only regularly day-flying member of the Footman group to occur in Britain and Ireland, and it also flies at night. The name footman was chosen because the folded wings are said to resemble the long, stiff coat worn by Victorian footmen. This is a resident species but it is thought that the population may be augmented by occasional immigrants. It occurs in mature woodland and is generally seen on hot, sunny days, particularly in areas where lichens and algae, the caterpillars' foodplants, can be found growing on the bark of old trees. Although they often settle on scrub at low level, sometimes in mating pairs, the adults are usually seen flying around the tops of tall trees, often oaks or spruces, sometimes swarming in considerable numbers.

The Red-necked Footman overwinters as a pupa in a silky cocoon formed among lichen and plant debris. Its caterpillars, which feed from July to October, are grey with dusky-yellow and red markings and brown hairs. Adult moths emerge in June.

Widely distributed although scarce except in south-west England, south-west Scotland and the west of Northern Ireland, where it can be locally abundant	
Where found:	Broad-leaved and mixed woodland, conifer plantations
When flying:	June–July
Forewing length:	14–18 mm
Larval foodplants:	Lichens and algae growing on mature trees

Similar species: None

A dorsal view showing the red neck that gives the species its name

×4 **Wood Tiger** *Parasemia plantaginis* 2056

The colour and pattern of this moth leave you in no doubt that it is in the tiger family. However, its name is misleading because, as well as being found in open areas within woodland, Wood Tigers frequently fly in open habitats like scrubby heathland, calcareous downland, moorlands and sand dunes – areas that often have no woods in sight! Although they occur locally throughout Britain, they are probably more likely to be seen in Scotland or Ireland. Males, in particular, fly fast in sunshine, on the lookout for newly emerged females sheltering in the grass. Whilst the general patterning on the wings is diagnostic, the ground-colour and markings can be quite variable, ranging from wholly dark hindwings (usually in females) to white (in males). The latter is form *hospita* and is fairly frequent in northern areas. In the far north of Scotland both sexes of the subspecies *insularum* have blacker hindwings with orangey markings.

The caterpillars eat a range of plants, such as Bell Heather, Ribwort Plantain and Common Rock-rose, and overwinter while still small, low down in vegetation. They are fully grown by late April and pupate in a cocoon spun among plant stems. Fully grown caterpillars are blackish with tufts of mostly black hairs except for three pairs of reddish tufts.

Priority Species (Northern Ireland)	
Fairly scarce, except in Scotland and Ireland; very scarce in south-east England	
Where found:	Open areas in woodland, scrubby heathland, moorland, calcareous grassland, sand dunes etc.
When flying:	May–July
Forewing length:	17–20 mm
Larval foodplants:	Herbaceous plants, such as Bell Heather, plantains, Common Rock–rose, Groundsel

Similar species: None

×3 **Jersey Tiger** *Euplagia quadripunctaria* 2067

As its name implies, the Jersey Tiger is commonly found throughout the Channel Islands. However, it can be found along the south coast of England, from east Devon to Portland, where there are many colonies. There are also a few colonies further inland, including one that was discovered in the Forest Hill area of London in 2004 and has since spread. It seems likely that the population is reinforced by immigrants from continental Europe, but the extent of any immigration is not known.

Jersey Tigers are unmistakable large, colourful moths with black-and-white forewings and brightly coloured hindwings (which may be red, orange or yellow). Adults will sometimes fly by day and occasionally have been seen feeding at buddleia or sitting on buildings. They rest low down in vegetation, from which they are easily disturbed. Their colourful, hairy caterpillars are blackish-brown with creamy markings and pale-brown hairs protruding from light-brown warts. They feed on Common Nettle and other herbaceous plants and hibernate during the winter while still very small.

Nationally Scarce B	
Common in the Channel Islands; scarce and local in southern England	
Where found:	Anywhere with flowers: gardens, allotments, waste ground, hedgerows, cliffs, vegetated shingle beaches
When flying:	Late July–September
Forewing length:	27–33 mm
Larval foodplants:	Common Nettle, Dandelion, plantains and other herbaceous plants

Similar species: None

×3 **Scarlet Tiger** *Callimorpha dominula* 2068

Scarlet Tigers are quite large and unmistakable moths, which in good years may find their way into gardens and suburban areas. However, their main habitats are fenland, marshy grassland, river banks, vegetated shingle and sand dunes.

When newly emerged, the dark areas of their forewings have a metallic-green sheen. Although the extent and shape of the white and yellow markings can vary slightly in detail, there is usually little variation. Both sexes are often found at rest on leaves, but males sometimes fly vigorously, particularly towards the end of the day. Unlike many moths in the family Arctiidae that do not have a functioning tongue, and therefore do not feed, this species is able to drink nectar from flowers.

There is one generation each year. The caterpillars hatch in July and feed on a wide range of herbaceous plants, particularly Common Comfrey. Like others of this family, they hibernate when quite small and resume feeding in the spring. They are black and hairy, marked with yellow and white overlapping spots, and may be encountered feeding or wandering over open ground looking for a good place to pupate. They spin a silken cocoon among plant debris, usually close to the ground.

Locally common in southern and south-west England, the south Midlands and Wales; very local in south-east England	
Where found:	Damp sites, fens, marshes, river banks, vegetated shingle
When flying:	June–July
Forewing length:	22–26 mm
Larval foodplants:	Usually Common Comfrey but disperses to feed on a range of other plants

Similar species: Cream-spot Tiger *Arctia villica*, but that species does not fly during the day

×3 **Ruby Tiger** *Phragmatobia fuliginosa*  2064

The Ruby Tiger is a common, small moth that can be found almost anywhere. It flies in many open habitats, including downland, heathland, moorland, sand dunes, woodland clearings and gardens. Newly emerged moths are a dark rosy-red with a pink abdomen and pink hindwings, though these scales are quickly lost, which leads to a duller appearance. There are usually two generations, but only one in Scotland, where most moths are of the ssp. *borealis,* which are darker in colour than those found further south.

First-generation moths are more likely to be seen during the day, as well as at night, when sometimes mating pairs are found. In contrast, second-generation moths seem reluctant to fly during the day but are regularly attracted to light at night.

Batches of eggs are laid on the leaves of many different foodplants. The caterpillars change colour as they mature, and when fully grown are black with copious golden-brown hairs. Second-brood caterpillars hibernate through the winter, only pupating in a cocoon near the ground in late spring.

Common and widespread over much of Britain and Ireland	
Where found:	Any open habitats, including gardens
When flying:	Mid-April–September and occasionally October in the south (two generations); May–July in the north (one generation)
Forewing length:	14–19 mm
Larval foodplants:	A range of herbaceous including ragworts and plantains, as well as Broom and other shrubby plants

Similar species: None

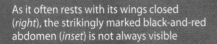
As it often rests with its wings closed (*right*), the strikingly marked black-and-red abdomen (*inset*) is not always visible

×3 # Cinnabar

Tyria jacobaeae 2069

The distinctive red and black pattern of the Cinnabar makes it easily recognizable. Only the burnet moths (*pages 33–39*) have similar colours, but they are quite different in appearance, having narrower wings and club-like antennae. Cinnabars frequent long grass, where they sometimes fly on sunny days, and from where they are often disturbed. Although there is only one generation, there is a long flight season, stretching from May to August. Rarely, genetic variations occur: in f. *flavescens* the red is replaced by yellow; in f. *coneyi* the forewings are completely red except for a black border; and in f. *negrana* all wings are wholly black.

Sometimes, in late August, adult moths may be seen flying alongside fully grown caterpillars. These have distinctive orange and black hoops (see *page 135*) and feed openly during the day, usually on Common Ragwort. Sometimes, complete plants will be stripped of their leaves, leaving only the stalks standing. The caterpillars climb down to pupate in a cocoon in or just below loose debris on the ground, where they spend the winter.

Legislative listing: NERC Act (S41 & S42)

Priority Species (Northern Ireland)

UK BAP Priority Species

Fairly common throughout England, Wales and Ireland; more local in Scotland, usually near the coast

Where found:	Well-drained grassland habitats, sand dunes, vegetated shingle, heathland and other open habitats, including woodland rides
When flying:	May–August, occasionally from late April and into October
Forewing length:	16–23 mm
Larval foodplants:	Common Ragwort, occasionally on other ragworts, Groundsel etc.

Similar species: Burnet moths (*pages 33–39*)

×3 **Clouded Buff** *Diacrisia sannio* `2059`

An unmistakable species. Males are slightly larger, lighter and brighter than females, which are a tawny-brown colour. The difference in appearance between the two sexes is so marked that they were once thought to be different species. In warm sunshine, males fly frequently during the day, as well as at night, and they are easily disturbed from resting in grass and low vegetation. As females fly mainly at night they are harder to find, but can occasionally be found at rest. The Clouded Buff is most frequent in southern Britain but is also found locally throughout most of England and Wales, northwards as far as western Scotland and in Ireland. It is usually found on heathland and moorland though it occasionally occurs on calcareous downland and in open areas in woodland.

♂♀

Although there are two broods in southern Europe, there is usually only one brood in the British Isles. Eggs are laid on low plants and the hairy caterpillars, which are grey with reddish-brown and light markings, emerge in July. They feed on Heather and a range of herbaceous plants and overwinter while still small, completing their development in late spring before pupating in a flimsy cocoon low down or on the ground.

Locally common in England; rarer in Wales, Scotland and Ireland	
Where found:	Moorland, heathland, bogs, calcareous grassland, open woodland and rough grassland
When flying:	June–August
Forewing length:	19–22 mm (males) 17–20 mm (females)
Larval foodplants:	Heather and low herbaceous plants, such as plantains and Devil's–bit Scabious

Similar species: None

Male

Female

×3 **Muslin Moth**   *Diaphora mendica* 2063

Like the Clouded Buff, this is an unusual moth because the two sexes look completely different. Males are grey-brown (except for those in Ireland, which are lighter and creamy-brown) in contrast to the females which have almost white and slightly translucent wings that resemble fine muslin cloth, hence the species' name. Both sexes have similarly spaced dark spots on their wings. Curiously, females are more likely to be found than males, because unlike many other species they sometimes fly in bright, sunny weather, whereas males generally only fly at night. Muslin Moths can be found almost anywhere and can sometimes be seen settled on low vegetation.

There is one generation, with adult moths on the wing from April to June. The caterpillars feed on a range of mainly low-growing herbaceous plants and complete their growth by September. By this time they have matured to a brownish-grey colour with paler markings and brown hairs. They spin a cocoon in plant debris on the ground, where they pupate to pass the winter.

Common in England and Wales; more local but widely distributed in Scotland and Ireland	
Where found:	Open habitats, including gardens, downland, woodland clearings
When flying:	April–early June
Forewing length:	14–17 mm (males) 17–19 mm (females)
Larval foodplants:	Docks, chickweeds and other low-growing plants

Similar species: White Ermine *Spilosoma lubricipeda*, Buff Ermine *S. luteum*, Water Ermine *S. urticae* but all these species are slightly larger and usually not day-flyers

Female

Male

147

Family: Noctuidae

Approximately 400 British species
26 day-flying

There are upwards of 21,000 members of the noctuid family worldwide. About 400 species are found in Britain and Ireland and, of these, 26 are regarded as day-flyers. They include locally common moths such as the Burnet Companion and Mother Shipton, which fly in the same habitat as Dingy Skipper butterflies, with which they are sometimes confused.

Probably the commonest of the day-flying noctuids is the Silver Y, which can appear just about anywhere from May to September, and occasionally at other times of the year. Silver Ys may be seen dashing about in a garden or over rough ground, flying quickly from place to place, though seldom lingering long. There are also some rare day-flying noctuids, such as the Four-spotted and the Silurian. To see these species you will have to explore areas where they are known to occur, and will probably need good luck if you are to be successful.

Preferred larval foodplants for the day-flying noctuids include grasses, clovers, bedstraws and some other herbaceous plants. Some caterpillars of the (many) night flyers in this family feed on the foliage of trees and woody plants, but those of the day-flyers prefer to keep nearer the ground. They then pupate on or below ground or within leaf-litter on the ground surface.

All but two of the day-flying species covered in this section breed in Britain and Ireland and are treated as resident moths. The population of a few of these species is reinforced by regular immigrations from Europe. Only two immigrants, the Bordered Straw and the Silver Y, are thought not to survive our winters. Their populations rely entirely upon the arrival of immigrant moths each spring. Both species breed, their caterpillars feeding on herbaceous and low-growing plants, the Silver Y having several generations during the summer.

In their usual resting position, noctuids fold their wings back over their bodies. The trailing edges of their forewings come together and sometimes overlap, the closed wings forming a tent-like shape over the body. In some species there are pronounced tufts standing up over the thorax, the Silver Y being a good example.

Silver Y drinking nectar from lavender

Day-flying noctuids favour heathland, moorland and open woodland

Night-flying noctuids that may be encountered during the day

In addition to the 26 noctuid species described here, there are several very common night-flyers. Occasionally, these may be disturbed from rest or found seeking nectar in the late afternoon. A light trap run overnight in August can attract a great number of Large Yellow Underwings *Noctua pronuba*. If this species, or another member of the same genus, is disturbed from vegetation during the day, it will fly rapidly for cover displaying a flash of its brightly coloured yellow hindwings. Although it will quickly disappear, it is a large moth (FL: 18–20 mm) and is easily seen.

Another resident and mainly night-flying noctuid, which is common throughout much of England and Wales and may occasionally be found during the day, is the beautiful Red Underwing *Catocala nupta*. This is very large (FL: 35–40 mm) and may sometimes be found resting on a wall or post during the day. It is mainly active at dusk, but has been found nectaring on Buddleia in afternoon sunshine. Also there are several other, rarer members of the genus *Catocala* that behave in a similar way. When disturbed, they fly away vigorously.

The large and stunning
Red Underwing
Catocala nupta

The striking hindwings of the **Large Yellow Underwing** *Noctua pronuba* are usually hidden when at rest (*top*), but very noticeable when it takes flight (*bottom*)

149

True Lover's Knot

×4

Lycophotia porphyrea **2118**

This small, attractive moth is quite common and may occur in large numbers on suitable habitat. It favours areas where heathers grow, particularly on high moors and heathland, but can occasionally wander more widely and visit gardens and woodlands. It can be quite active in bright sunlight, settling to drink nectar from heather flowers. There are two other species of moth that occur in the same habitat as True Lover's Knot that are superficially similar and can be difficult to separate: the Beautiful Yellow Underwing and Heath Rustic *Xestia agathina*. However, although the flight periods of these three species could potentially overlap, the Beautiful Yellow Underwing tends to be on the wing earlier in the year than True Lover's Knot, and the Heath Rustic usually flies rather later in the year and not during the day.

There is one generation and Heather and Bell Heather are the caterpillars' main foodplants. The caterpillars are reddish-brown with a prominent pale line along their back flanked by black markings, and with lighter markings along their sides. They overwinter when almost fully grown but, after the winter, continue feeding until as late as May. They pupate in a cocoon on or just below the ground surface.

Common and widespread, sometimes numerous in suitable localities	
Where found:	Heathlands and moorland, sometimes gardens and open woodland
When flying:	June–August
Forewing length:	12–15 mm
Larval foodplants:	Heather and Bell Heather, probably also Cross-leaved Heath

Similar species: Beautiful Yellow Underwing, Heath Rustic *Xestia agathina* (although the latter usually only flies at dusk, after the sun has gone down)

× 4 **Beautiful Yellow Underwing** *Anarta myrtilli* 2142

This little moth flies rapidly backwards and forwards over heathers on heathland and moorlands, stopping to feed on any convenient flower. In dull weather it can often be found resting on heathers. Several moths have yellow underwings, including Small Dark Yellow Underwing (*page 152*), but the Beautiful Yellow Underwing can be distinguished by the fact that it has reddish-brown forewings with a conspicuous small central white blotch. The True Lover's Knot is also a potential confusion species, but it does not have colourful hindwings and the flight periods do not normally overlap.

There are thought to be two generations in the south, where the flight period is longer than in the north. Caterpillars are olive-green marbled with white and yellow and with a green head. They feed openly during the day on the terminal shoots of Heather and Bell Heather. Curiously for such a common moth, it is not known whether overwintering takes place in the larval or pupal stage. Pupation occurs within a tough cocoon formed in plant litter on or just below the ground surface.

Local, but can be fairly common in suitable habitat	
Where found:	Heathland and moorland throughout Britain and Ireland
When flying:	Late April–August
Forewing length:	10–12mm
Larval foodplants:	Heather and Bell Heather

Similar species: Small Dark Yellow Underwing (*page 152*), True Lover's Knot

× 4 **Small Dark Yellow Underwing**   *Anarta cordigera* 2143

The Small Dark Yellow Underwing is a rare moth, found only in Scotland. When at rest it can be difficult to identify, as several other species in the family Noctuidae look similar. However, if yellow underwings can be seen, and you are on heathland or moorland, it must then be either this species or a Beautiful Yellow Underwing (*page 151*). There is not much difference in size, but the latter usually has a reddish tinge and more extensive white markings. A feature that distinguishes the Small Dark Yellow Underwing is the prominent white 'kidney mark' on each forewing. The Small Yellow Underwing (*page 154*) also has yellow underwings but occurs in a different habitat (flowery grasslands) and is much smaller.

Adults fly rapidly in sunshine. They seem to prefer stony ground at relatively low altitudes (up to 650 m (2,130 ft) has been suggested) and may sometimes be found settled on the ground or on posts. They may be expected over their caterpillars' foodplant, Bearberry, whereas Beautiful Yellow Underwings fly over heather, but as both plants often grow together, this does not aid identification. Caterpillars of this species are dark reddish-brown with whitish markings. Unlike those of the Beautiful Yellow Underwing, they feed at night. They pass the winter as pupa inside a cocoon on the ground, from which the next generation emerges in late spring.

Nationally Rare	
Scottish Biodiversity List	
UK BAP Priority Species	
Mostly recorded from the central highlands of Scotland; seemingly declining	

Where found:	Moorland
When flying:	Late April– mid-June
Forewing length:	10–12 mm
Larval foodplant:	Bearberry

Similar species: Beautiful Yellow Underwing (*page 151*), Small Yellow Underwing (*page 162*) and, when settled, several other noctuids

×4 **Broad-bordered White Underwing** *Anarta melanopa* **2144**

Found only in Scotland, the Broad-bordered White Underwing is a rather local, usually, high-altitude species. There is, however, one English record from the Cheviots in Northumberland in 1974. Its preferred habitat is open moorland above about 600 m (2,000 ft), but it has been found at lower altitudes in the far north. It can sometimes be seen flying fast, close to the ground, and stopping periodically to visit the flowers of low-growing shrubby plants such as Crowberry and Bilberry. It is active on both sunny and dull days, provided that the weather is warm.

The forewings are greyish-brown marked with black and have no central white spot, and the hindwings are black and white, lacking any yellow. The combination of these characters means that the Broad-bordered White Underwing is unlikely to be confused with other similar noctuids, such as the Beautiful Yellow Underwing (*page 151*) and Small Dark Yellow Underwing.

The caterpillars, which are reported to be purplish-pink with mainly reddish-brown markings, feed at night on a range of moorland plants, such as Cowberry, Crowberry, Bearberry and Bilberry. Like the Small Dark Yellow Underwing, there is one generation, with caterpillars pupating in early autumn in a cocoon on the ground, where they pass the winter.

Rare, found only in Scotland (except for one record in Northumberland)	
Where found:	Highlands and southern uplands of Scotland
When flying:	May–June
Forewing length:	11–13 mm
Larval foodplants:	Cowberry, Crowberry, Bearberry, Bilberry

Similar species: Small Dark Yellow Underwing (also rare), Beautiful Yellow Underwing (*page 151*) (much commoner)

× 4 **Small Yellow Underwing** *Panemeria tenebrata* 2397

This small moth is active during sunny weather in the early summer, and is frequently seen on the wing visiting flowers in open grassy areas. When settled, its yellow underwings are usually visible. Localized colonies may occur almost anywhere, except in much of Scotland and Ireland. It is smaller, although otherwise somewhat similar to the Small Dark Yellow Underwing (*page 152*) and the same size as the Small Purple and Gold (*page 192*), which both fly during the day. However, it is unlikely to be confused with the Small Dark Yellow Underwing as that species has a more rounded shape and lives on high moorland. The Small Purple and Gold occurs in similar localities to the Small Yellow Underwing, but has redder forewings with at least one orange-yellow spot.

The caterpillars, which are green with whitish and yellow markings, bore into the unopened flower capsules of either Common or Field Mouse-ear and eat its flowers and seeds. Towards the end of the summer, they pupate in a cocoon just below the ground surface. There is one generation, with adults emerginge in May.

> Local throughout much of England and Wales; rarer in south-west Ireland and south-east Scotland, but possibly overlooked

Where found:	Flowery meadows, woodland edges, hedgerows, calcareous grassland
When flying:	Late April–early June
Forewing length:	8–10 mm
Larval foodplants:	Common Mouse-ear, Field Mouse-ear

Similar species: Small Dark Yellow Underwing (*page 152*), Small Purple and Gold (*page 192*)

×4 **Silurian** *Eriopygodes imbecilla* 2175

The Silurian was only discovered in the British Isles in 1972, in Wales. It favours high moorland with sheltered gullies and hollows, and although attracted to light at night, it is also known to fly in sunlight during the day. Only two breeding areas are currently known: one in the Brecon Beacons in Monmouthshire and the other in the Black Mountains on the England/Wales border. The name Silurian was chosen because the Brecon Beacons were once the domain of an iron-age tribe called the Silures.

The ground-colour of adult moths ranges from reddish-brown to fawn, with irregular shading and an indistinct 'kidney mark' on each forewing. Females are slightly smaller than males and may have a brighter 'kidney mark'. The caterpillars, which are pinkish-brown and feed at night on Bilberry or Heath Bedstraw, were only discovered in the wild in Britain in 2006. Since then, they have proven to be easier to find during April than the adult moths are in June and July. They pupate in the late spring.

Nationally Rare	
Legislative listing: NERC Act (S42)	
Very rare, only two breeding areas are known	
Where found:	High moorland in Wales and on the England/Wales border
When flying:	June–July
Forewing length:	10–13 mm
Larval foodplants:	Bilberry and Heath Bedstraw
Similar species: None	

× 4 **Cloaked Minor**   *Mesoligia furuncula*   **2341**

The Cloaked Minor is most likely to be encountered on sand dunes and grassy slopes near the coast, but is also found inland on grassy sites throughout Britain and Ireland. The name of this species conjures the image of a Victorian lady wearing a dark cloak over a full skirt. However, the moth's colours vary considerably and the dark 'cloak' may sometimes be so light that there is very little contrast between 'cloak' and 'skirt'. On the sand dunes of western Ireland and coastal Northumbria, a pale straw-coloured form *latristiata* occurs in which the cloak effect is not apparent. Although it is usually on the wing after dark, this species occasionally flies in sunshine and may be found at rest on the flowers of plants such as Marram and Common Ragwort. The Least Minor could potentially be confused with this species but, as its name implies, is smaller.

The caterpillars are pinkish-ochre with reddish-brown markings and feed on a range of grasses. They have a long life, hatching in August, overwintering and then resuming feeding until fully grown in June. They feed inside the stems of grass, gradually eating their way downwards to pupate in the base of their foodplant during the summer.

Fairly common	
Where found:	Grassy areas, such as downland, embankments, verges, coastal cliffs, sand dunes; most frequent on coastal sites
When flying:	Late July–September
Forewing length:	10–12 mm
Larval foodplants:	Grasses, including Sheep's Fescue, Tufted Hair-grass, False Oat-grass

Similar species: Least Minor, Rosy Minor *Mesoligia literosa*, Small Dotted Buff *Photedes minima* and Small Wainscot *Chortodes pygmina*, although only the Least Minor flies regularly during the day

The intensity of the dark 'cloak' is variable

×4 **Least Minor**   *Photedes captiuncula* **2344**

The Least Minor is one of the smallest noctuids found in Britain and Ireland, and it is also smaller than some micro-moths. It is very scarce and found only locally on limestone grassland in southern Cumbria, northern Yorkshire, Northumberland and Durham (where it is largely coastal), and in western Ireland. Males in particular are very flighty and are easily disturbed by the slightest movement of the vegetation. They can then be seen flying about rapidly in the sunshine before diving down to settle in the grass again. The subspecies *tincta* found in Ireland is redder than the British subspecies *expolita* (illustrated).

Least Minor is only likely to be confused with the Cloaked Minor, but is smaller and lacks the 'cloak' that is usually evident in that species.

The small, dull, putty-coloured caterpillars have a reddish tinge. They live inside the stems of Glaucous Sedge, and possibly other sedges, and have a long life, overwintering before resuming feeding, and then pupating in a cocoon on the ground late the following May.

Nationally Rare	
Scarce, only found locally in the north of England and western Ireland	
Where found:	Limestone grassland, rough fields, cliff tops
When flying:	Late May–early August
Forewing length:	7–9 mm
Larval foodplants:	Within the stems of Glaucous Sedge and possibly other sedges

Similar species: Cloaked Minor

× 4 **Antler Moth** *Cerapteryx graminis* 2176

The central, pale, forked streak on the forewings of this medium-sized moth, said to resemble the antler of a stag, is diagnostic. Both sexes fly by day and at night, and can often be seen flying over grass and heather growing on high ground. Adults are sometimes found on flowerheads, such as those of thistles and ragworts. There is considerable variation in ground-colour, which ranges from light olive-brown to reddish-brown, and the extent and depth of colour of the black markings are variable. This species occurs widely in Britain, with numbers fluctuating from year to year, occasionally being abundant.

The female scatters her eggs over grassland and they do not hatch until the following spring. The glossy bronzy-brown caterpillars can occasionally occur in large numbers on grassy hills from March to June. When this is the case, the grasses can sometimes be stripped bare. Although caterpillars feed mainly at night, hiding in the grass during the day, they still prove a great attraction to birds. But enough always survive to ensure that the next generation of moths appears in good numbers in late summer.

Common and widely distributed, particularly in northern upland areas	
Where found:	Open grasslands, such as downland and upland moorland
When flying:	July–September
Forewing length:	12–17 mm
Larval foodplants:	Grasses, including Sheep's Fescue, Purple Moor-grass, Mat-grass, and possibly various sedges and rushes

Similar species: None

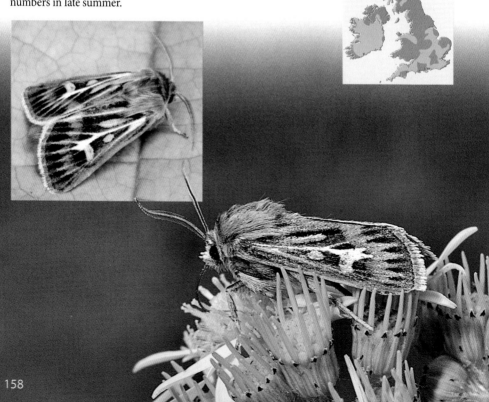

×4 **Dusky Sallow**   *Eremobia ochroleuca*   2352

The dark, broken band across the forewing of the Dusky Sallow is distinctive, and it is unlikely to be confused with any other species. It flies during the day (and at night) in July and August, when it can be found resting or feeding on flowers, particularly knapweeds, growing in a wide range of habitats including grassland, heathland, scrub, open woodland and sand dunes and vegetated shingle on the coast. This species is widely distributed in the south-east and East Anglia, but is rarely seen further north than Yorkshire or in the far south-west.

The Dusky Sallow has one generation each year. Eggs are laid in late summer and overwinter before hatching in April. The caterpillars, which are glossy pale-green with mainly whitish markings, feed on the flowers and seeds of many different grasses. After about three months, they crawl down to burrow just below the ground surface, where they spin a cocoon and pupate. Adult moths emerge quite late in the season, usually towards the end of July.

Widely distributed and sometimes common in the south-east and East Anglia; rare elsewhere	
Where found:	Open chalk grassland and many other grassy habitats, including coastal shingle, waste ground and woodland rides
When flying:	July–August
Forewing length:	14–16 mm
Larval foodplants:	Cock's-foot, False Oat-grass, Common Couch and other grasses, and sometimes cereal crops
Similar species: None	

×4 **Ear Moth**

Amphipoea oculea **2360**

The Ear Moth is a small, rather nondescript moth with an ear-like marking on each forewing. It is common throughout much of Britain and Ireland, although typically only found in small numbers. Sometimes, it visits flowers, such as thistles and ragworts, for nectar during the day. This species may be encountered almost anywhere, with damp, uncultivated grassland being favoured. There are three closely related species (see *similar species*) that were originally thought to be different forms of the Ear Moth. They are near identical in appearance and microscopic examination of their genitalia is needed to distinguish them with certainty.

The caterpillars of the Ear Moth are greenish-pink with grey and brown markings, and eat the lower stems of grasses. Adults fly in one generation, laying their eggs at the end of the summer. These hatch the following spring and, after three months, the caterpillars are fully grown and pupate underground in the roots of grasses.

Legislative listing: NERC Act (S41 & S42)

Priority Species (Northern Ireland)

UK BAP Priority Species (research)

Common and widespread but usually in low numbers

Where found:	Woodland rides, rough grassland, moorland, gardens
When flying:	Late July–September
Forewing length:	12–15 mm
Larval foodplants:	Grasses, including meadow-grasses and Tufted Hair-grass

Similar species: Large Ear *Amphipoea lucens*, Crinan Ear *A. crinanensis*, Saltern Ear *A. fucosa* (all of which are less common, except in Ireland where the Crinan Ear is the most frequent of the 'ear' moths)

× 4 **Haworth's Minor** *Celaena haworthii* 2367

This is a small moth that is commoner in the north of Britain than in the south, and is local in Ireland. It is reddish-brown with conspicuous white 'kidney' marks on each forewing. These have thin white streaks extending towards the outer edge of each wing, and sometimes in the opposite direction towards the base. Both sexes fly at night and males also fly on sunny afternoons, usually towards the end of the day, when they may stop to feed on flowers. They are mainly found on the moors and mosses of north Wales and northern England, Scotland and Ireland. Although Haworth's Minor was discovered on the Cambridgeshire fens many years ago, it is scarce and local throughout the East Anglian fens and broads, and very local in parts of southern England and south Wales.

The caterpillars feed on Common Cotton-grass and possibly other related wetland plants. They are purplish-brown with pale markings and are not often seen because they bore into plant stems and then remain out of sight until emerging to form a pupa low down at the base of their foodplant. There is one generation, with eggs laid in the early autumn not hatching until late the following spring.

Legislative listing: NERC Act (S41 & S42)	
Priority Species (Northern Ireland)	
UK BAP Priority Species (research)	
Widespread in the north and west of Britain, very local in the south; localized in Ireland	

Where found:	Damp moorland, marshes, fenland
When flying:	August–September
Forewing length:	10–14 mm
Larval foodplants:	Common Cotton-grass and possibly rushes and club-rushes

Similar species: The Crescent *Celaena leucostigma*, although this is larger and does not usually fly by day except in Scotland where the small Scottish subspecies *scotica* is sometimes active

× 4 **Marbled Clover** *Heliothis viriplaca* **2401**

The national strongholds of this rare moth are the dry heathlands and field margins of the Brecks of East Anglia. It dashes about rapidly during the day, regularly settling on flowers. Viper's-bugloss is a favourite but many other common flowers are visited, including Red Clover. It is also found very locally on flowery chalk downland in central southern England and on vegetated shingle and sand dunes, but is much less frequent in these habitats. The resident population is occasionally reinforced by immigrants from the continent.

The intensity of colour and markings of the Marbled Clover are variable but it is only likely to be confused with the Shoulder-striped Clover.

The caterpillars are also variable in colour, and can be different shades of green or purplish-brown with whitish or yellow markings. They feed on the flowers and seeds of many different plants. Sometimes, there is a partial second generation, but mature caterpillars pupate before the winter in a cocoon on or just below the ground. Adult moths emerge at the height of summer and have quite a short flight season.

Nationally Rare	
Sometimes locally common in East Anglia, but scarce and very local elsewhere	
Where found:	Dry heathland, chalk downland, sand dunes, vegetated shingle
When flying:	June–July, sometimes into August
Forewing length:	14–16 mm
Larval foodplants:	A wide range of low-growing herbaceous plants

Similar species: Shoulder-striped Clover

Marbled Clover has a 'kink' in the front edge of the dark band across the forewings that is much less pronounced than that of the Shoulder-striped Clover

×4 Shoulder-striped Clover

Heliothis maritima 2402

The Shoulder-striped Clover is very rare, now occurring only at a few localized sites on damp heathland in Surrey, Hampshire and Dorset, where it flies fast in hot sunshine, stopping occasionally to drink nectar from heathland flowers. Although similar in appearance to the Marbled Clover, the Shoulder-striped Clover has a short, narrow dark streak where the forewing is attached to the thorax, although this is sometimes indistinct. It also has a more acute 'kink' in the front edge of the dark band that runs across the centre of the forewings, towards the leading edge.

Although the appearance and life history of the caterpillars of the two species are very similar, their foodplants are different. The caterpillars of Shoulder-striped Clover favour heathland plants, feeding on the flowers and seeds of Cross-leaved Heath, Heather and Bog Asphodel, whereas the Marbled Clover prefers to feed on herbaceous plants growing on calcareous soils. However, very rarely, immigrants of both these species arrive in the British Isles from continental Europe, and they can then often be found in unexpected places.

Nationally Rare	
Legislative listing: NERC Act (S41)	
UK BAP Priority Species	
Very rare. only found on a few acid heaths in southern England	

Where found:	Open heathland
When flying:	June–July
Forewing length:	13–17 mm
Larval foodplants:	Mainly Cross-leaved Heath, also Heather, Bog Asphodel

Similar species: Marbled Clover

The short, narrow streak and more acute 'kink' in the dark band distinguish the Shoulder-striped Clover from the Marbled Clover

× 4 **Bordered Straw** *Heliothis peltigera* 2403

The Bordered Straw is an immigrant that travels all the way from the Mediterranean, usually arriving in the British Isles between June and August. Its ground-colour is variable and sometimes quite pale, and there is a suggestion that pale moths have come from desert regions. The numbers vary considerably from year to year, and in some years this species can be quite common round the coast of southern England and Wales, and it may also arrive anywhere in Britain and Ireland. In other years, it can be very scarce. It flies in sunshine as well as at night, and can be found feeding from flowers during the day. Confusion is possible with two other immigrant species that sometimes turn up in Britain, the Scarce Bordered Straw *Helicoverpa armigera* and Eastern Bordered Straw *Heliothis nubigera*.

The caterpillars are predominantly green, with red and whitish markings. They feed on the flowers of many different herbaceous plants, sometimes including garden marigolds. Although caterpillars have been found between June and October, occasionally in numbers, there is no evidence that they are able to survive the winter in Britain and Ireland.

Immigrant, particularly to southern England and Wales; can be fairly common in some years	
Where found:	Flowery coastal habitats, such as dunes and vegetated shingle, but can occur almost anywhere
When flying:	Usually June–August, although occasionally outside this period
Forewing length:	16–19 mm
Larval foodplants:	Common Restharrow, Scentless Mayweed, Sticky Groundsel and many other plants including garden marigolds

Similar species: Scarce Bordered Straw *Helicoverpa armigera* and Eastern Bordered Straw *Heliothis nubigera* are also immigrants but are usually rarer than the Bordered Straw; they lack the distinct black dot at the trailing corner of the Bordered Straw's forewings

×4 **Northern Rustic** *Standfussiana lucernea* `2104`

Although the Northern Rustic usually flies at night, it will also readily fly during the day if it is sunny, particularly in the late afternoon. It is predominantly a coastal species in Wales, western Scotland, north-west England, and Ireland, and very locally in southern England. However, it may also be found inland in parts of Wales, northern England and Scotland and shows a preference for areas of sparse vegetation, such as on cliffs, loose rocky ground and quarries.

The moth's ground-colour varies from grey-brown to slate-grey. Its markings are generally indistinct but, when seen, the hindwings particularly have prominent white fringes. Colonies on Shetland tend to be larger and darker than elsewhere, with their forewings almost blue-black.

There is only one generation a year. The caterpillars are a mottled olive-green with black markings, and are not at all fussy about what they eat; they have been found feeding on many different herbaceous plants as well as various grasses. Caterpillars overwinter while still small, low down near the ground, and pupate in the late spring.

Widespread but fairly local	
Where found:	West coast of England, Wales, Ireland and northern Scotland; locally inland in Wales and northern England
When flying:	July–September
Forewing length:	16–21 mm
Larval foodplants:	Many different herbaceous plants including Harebell, Biting Stonecrop, saxifrages; grasses

Similar species: Dotted Rustic *Rhyacia simulans*, Stout Dart *Spaelotis ravida*, The Grey *Hadena caesia*, but these do not usually fly by day

× 4 **Silver Hook** *Deltote uncula* 2412

This distinctive, small moth takes its name from the hook-like mark on each forewing. It flies at night, but also by day whenever it is disturbed from resting in tussocks of grass. Although the number of moths in a colony is usually small, the Silver Hook occurs widely, but locally, on marshy habitat throughout Britain and Ireland, except for the central counties of England and eastern Scotland. The fenlands of East Anglia, in particular, are probably one of the best places to look for this species. Their usual flight season is late May to early July. However, they are occasionally found in August, and it is thought that these individuals may be the result of there being a second (summer) generation, but that is still uncertain.

Caterpillars are green with whitish-yellow markings. They feed on sedges and coarse grasses, burrowing below the ground surface to pupate in a strong cocoon. Usually, caterpillars pupate in the early autumn, with adult moths not emerging until the following May.

Scattered locally throughout Britain and Ireland, except central England and eastern Scotland	
Where found:	Fens, marshes, boggy heathland, water-logged meadows, damp moorland
When flying:	May–July, occasionally August
Forewing length:	10–12 mm
Larval foodplants:	Sedges and grasses
Similar species: None	

×4 **Silver Barred**   *Deltote bankiana* 2413

The Silver Barred is an extremely scarce moth that occurs at a very limited number of sites, although it can sometimes be found in numbers. It is well known from Wicken Fen and Chippenham Fen in Cambridgeshire and various peat bogs in south-west Ireland. Small colonies have also been found extremely locally on the coast in Kent, possibly as a result of immigration from continental Europe.

This species is identified by the presence of silvery-white parallel lines running at a slight angle across the forewings; individuals from Ireland tend to be slightly redder and a little larger. It often sits openly on vegetation during the day, and is easily disturbed, even in dull weather, when it flies for a short while before settling again. Otherwise it is normally active after dusk, when it may be attracted to light.

The yellowish-green caterpillars feed at night from June to August on a range of different grasses, with Purple Moor-grass tussocks being a particular favourite. They pupate before the winter in a cocoon low down among the roots, with the next generation emerging in early May. There may be a partial second generation during the summer, when the whole life-cycle is reduced from a year to just a few months so that the second-generation caterpillars have time to pupate before the winter.

British Red Data Book (Vulnerable)	
Common in two localized fenland sites in Cambridgeshire, and in peat bogs in south-west Ireland. Has also been found very locally on the coast of Kent	
Where found:	Fens, marshes and boggy heathland
When flying:	May–July, sometimes August
Forewing length:	10–12 mm
Larval foodplants:	Grasses, including Purple Moor-grass and meadow-grasses
Similar species: None	

×4 # Silver Y

Autographa gamma **2441**

The Silver Y, one of the most commonly seen day-flying moths, is an immigrant from continental Europe. Coastal sites are good places to search for this species, where thousands can sometimes be seen together, but it can occur almost anywhere. There can be several generations a year and, as spring arrivals often breed, and these are then supplemented by later-arriving immigrants, by autumn the population can be large. They are frequently seen by day, flying frantically as they visit flowers, as well as at dusk, and at night.

The Silver Y is named after the well-defined, continuous 'Y'-mark on its forewing. Its relative, the Scarce Silver Y usually has a broken 'Y'-mark, has silvery-grey markings on a black ground-colour, and tends to be smaller.

The caterpillars take only about a month to become fully grown and vary a great deal in appearance, from pale green to dark olive-green, with paler markings. They will eat almost any low-growing vegetation, whether wild or cultivated. They feed at night and pupate in a flimsy cocoon, with their dark pupa clearly visible, spun between the folds of a leaf. Generally, the immature stages do not survive the winter, but caterpillars have occasionally been found in February. Adult moths have been seen in every month of the year. During the winter, they are thought to have been brought by mild southerly winds sweeping them up from the continent.

Common immigrant, numbers varying considerably from year to year	
Where found:	Particularly at coastal locations where incoming immigrants gather; sometimes on garden flowers and plants
When flying:	April–October, rarely other months
Forewing length:	13–22 mm
Larval foodplants:	Many different low-growing plants, including bedstraws, clovers, nettles, peas, cabbages, runner beans

Similar species: Several, including the Scarce Silver Y and the Ni Moth *Trichoplusia ni* (although this has the silver mark broken in two and is not usually a day-flyer)

×4 **Scarce Silver Y** *Syngrapha interrogationis* `2447`

Although more usually flying at night, the Scarce Silver Y can sometimes be found on the wing in sunshine on moorland, mainly in the north of England, parts of Wales, Scotland and Ireland. However, the arrival of immigrants from continental Europe means that, very occasionally, it may potentially be found almost anywhere. Unlike its more commonly seen relative the Silver Y, the ground-colour of the Scarce Silver Y is usually blackish with silvery-grey markings, the 'Y'-marking is not as distinct and is often split, and the moth is usually slightly smaller than the Silver Y.

There are also several other similar species, the closest of which is the Ni Moth *Trichoplusia ni*, but these do not normally fly during the day.

The resident population of Scarce Silver Y has one generation a year, with caterpillars hatching from late July onwards. They are green, inclining to blackish, with white lines and markings. After hibernation during the winter, caterpillars resume feeding, usually on moorland Heather or Bilberry. Then, like the Silver Y, they spin a cocoon within their foodplant to enclose their dark-brown pupa. Adult moths emerge from late June. It is reported that parasitic flies regularly attack the caterpillars of this species.

Seen fairly frequently throughout northern Britain and Ireland and locally in Wales; elsewhere only occasional immigrants	
Where found:	Moorland
When flying:	June–August
Forewing length:	15–18mm
Larval foodplants:	Heather, Bilberry, Bog Bilberry

Similar species: Silver Y, and the Ni Moth *Trichoplusia ni* (lighter brown with the silver mark is broken in two; not usually a day-flyer)

×4 **Gold Spangle** *Autographa bractea* `2444`

The distinctive Gold Spangle takes its name from the large solid-looking gold mark on each forewing. This feature, although diagnostic, can sometimes vary slightly in shape. It is a common resident in the north of England, Wales, Scotland and Ireland, but is much scarcer in the English Midlands and further south. Its distribution in the southern part of its range has fluctuated over the years, the reasons for which are not understood, but recent records may involve immigrants or wanderers from northern colonies. It is found on moorland, in woodland, along hedgerows and verges, and in gardens, with a seeming preference for open habitats. There is one generation, with adult moths on the wing in late summer, when they sometimes fly by day and often feed on flowers at dusk.

The caterpillars are bright-green, spotted with white and with darker green markings. They feed on a wide range of plants, including Common Nettle and Ground-ivy, and overwinter while still small, resuming feeding in the spring. They pupate in May in a cocoon spun under a leaf of their chosen foodplant.

> In most years, common in Wales, northern England, Scotland and Ireland; much rarer in southern England, where it is thought possibly to be an immigrant

Where found:	May be anywhere but prefers more open habitats
When flying:	Late June–August
Forewing length:	18–21 mm
Larval foodplants:	Many different herbaceous plants, including Common Nettle, White Dead-nettle and Ground–ivy; also honeysuckles and Bilberry

Similar species: None

× 4 Four-spotted *Tyta luctuosa* **2465**

Although records indicate that the Four-spotted was once distributed more widely across southern England, East Anglia and parts of the Midlands, it is now rare and very localized. The populations that remain are on the Isle of Portland, in Kent, Northamptonshire and Bedfordshire, and on the Essex-Cambridgeshire border. This very pretty moth is named after the four patches of pinkish-white, one on each wing. It flies openly during the day, as well as at night, favouring warm, open areas with sparse vegetation, and can frequently be found resting in the flowers of its caterpillars' foodplant, Field Bindweed. There is usually only one generation a year, but on the Isle of Portland two regularly occur.

The caterpillars are brownish-grey with dark-edged lines and darker markings. They feed at night on Field Bindweed, hiding low down in vegetation during the day. Initially, they eat unopened flower buds but move on to the leaves as they mature. They overwinter as pupae. A peculiarity of this species is that it may appear in numbers on a site one year but be completely absent the following year. However, it may then be discovered at a new locality not far away. Flourishing Field Bindweed and recently disturbed ground appear to be two of the key habitat requirements for this species.

British Red Data Book (Vulnerable)	
Legislative listing: NERC Act (S41)	
UK BAP Priority Species	
Rare and localized, with few remaining populations	
Where found:	Warm, dry, open ground with sparse vegetation and broken soil
When flying:	May–August, sometimes to mid-September and rarely at the end of April
Forewing length:	12–13 mm
Larval foodplant:	Field Bindweed

Similar species: None except for a rare immigrant, the Pale Shoulder *Acontia lucida*, of which only a handful of specimens have ever been found here

×4 **Burnet Companion**   *Euclidia glyphica* 2463

The Burnet Companion is a relatively common, but localized, species that is often found in the company of other day-flying moths. As some of its 'companions' are often members of the Burnet family (Zygaenidae) (see *page 28*), this is how the species got its name. It can also be seen flying with Mother Shipton and the Dingy Skipper butterfly, which are potential confusion species. However, the Burnet Companion's unique combination of markings, and colourful hindwings are diagnostic. Burnet Companions are found widely across England, Wales, southern Scotland and Ireland but are most frequent in the south of England. As well as in sunshine, they also fly on dull days provided it is warm. If they are disturbed from shelter in long grass, they usually fly rapidly but only for a short distance before settling again.

There is one generation a year. The caterpillars, which are pale ochre-yellow with fine greyish-brown markings, do not appear to eat grasses, preferring instead clovers, trefoils and vetches. They feed at night before pupating at the beginning of autumn in a cocoon spun among plant debris.

Common in southern Britain; widespread but local elsewhere; rare in Scotland	
Where found:	Grasslands, usually on calcareous soils, including flowery meadows, downland, verges and woodland rides
When flying:	May–July
Forewing length:	12–15 mm
Larval foodplants:	Various vetches, trefoils and clovers, including Lucerne and Common Bird's-foot-trefoil

Similar species: Flies with Mother Shipton and Dingy Skipper butterfly, and may be confused with both

×4 Mother Shipton

Callistege mi 2462

The Mother Shipton is named after a real person, a prophetess who died in 1561. Legend claims she was ugly, and the dark markings on each forewing of this moth are said to resemble a profile of her head, with a long nose and beady eye. It flies in flower-rich grasslands, where it is often seen with the Burnet Companion and the Dingy Skipper butterfly. However, its distinctive markings, especially the 'face' on its forewings, are unique. The Mother Shipton flies rapidly, only for short distances, stopping occasionally on flowers, or 'hopping' low down in the grass from one hiding place to another.

There is one generation a year. The caterpillars are light pinkish-brown with whitish and darker-brown markings, and they eat clovers and other plants, including grasses, from late June to September. They feed at night, resting out of sight during the day, and pupate in a cocoon spun between blades of grass, where they remain dormant until the adult moths emerge the following May.

Common in England and Wales; scarcer in Scotland and Ireland

Where found:	Open grassland, heathland, moorland, woodland rides, roadside verges, embankments
When flying:	May–early July
Forewing length:	13–16 mm
Larval foodplants:	White, Red and Hare's-foot Clovers, Lucerne, Black Medick, Common Bird's-foot-trefoil and grasses

Similar species: Flies with Burnet Companion and Dingy Skipper butterfly

×4 **Blackneck** *Lygephila pastinum* **2466**

Blackneck is a good name for this moth, although perhaps Dark-brown Neck would have been more accurate! It is easily disturbed by day, and can often be seen at dusk fluttering over scrubby marshland or around the borders of woodlands. Although it is a localized species, it occurs throughout much of England and Wales, but tends to be more frequent in the south. The only species that is similar is Scarce Blackneck *Lygephila craccae*, which can sometimes also be disturbed during the day, especially in very hot weather. However, as this is a Nationally Rare species restricted to rocky coastal habitat in Devon, Cornwall, and one site in Somerset, the chances of confusion are small.

Blackneck caterpillars are yellowish-grey with reddish and black markings They feed at night on Tufted Vetch (Scarce Blackneck caterpillars feed on Wood Vetch) and hibernate during the winter. They reach maturity in May and pupate in a cocoon spun among plant stems and debris near or on the ground. There is one generation.

Locally common in southern Britain as far north as Yorkshire and Lancashire; rarer in Wales	
Where found:	Fens, marshes, scrubby damp woodland, dry calcareous grassland
When flying:	June–July
Forewing length:	17–21 mm
Larval foodplant:	Tufted vetch, occasionally Marsh Pea, Wild Liquorice

Similar species: Scarce Blackneck *Lygephila craccae* (FL: 20–23 mm), but this is confined to rocky coastal habitat in Devon, Cornwall and one coastal site in Somerset

The **Scarce Blackneck** (*inset*) is slightly stouter, has a series of blackish marks on the leading edge of its forewing, and usually flies slightly later in the summer (mid-July to mid-August).

×4 **Small Purple-barred** *Phytometra viridaria* **2470**

The name of this moth is a perfect description – it has two distinct pinkish-purple bars across its forewings that continue across the hindwings, and it is a small moth. However, it can be quite variable and in some forms (*e.g.* f. *fusca*) the purple bars almost disappear; the purple bars can also fade with age. The Small Purple-barred is a strong day-flyer on heathland, calcareous grassland and other open, flowery sites, particularly in the south of England, flitting from flower to flower in strong sunshine.

There is one generation each year, although there may be a partial second generation as this moth has been seen on the wing as late as August (it usually only flies into July). The caterpillars, which feed on milkworts, are green with pale yellowish and darker green markings and may be found from late June to September. They pupate low to the ground in cocoons formed among plant debris. Here they overwinter until the adult moths emerge in May.

Widely distributed in the south of England, more local elsewhere throughout Britain and Ireland	
Where found:	Heathland, moorland, calcareous grassland, open woodland, sand dunes
When flying:	May–July, sometimes into August
Forewing length:	9–11 mm
Larval foodplants:	Common Milkwort, Heath Milkwort

Similar species: May be confused with some micro-moths in the genus *Pyrausta*, such as the Small Purple and Gold (*page 192*)

MICRO-MOTHS

Approx. 1,600 British species
Many day-flying; a representative selection of 22 species illustrated

Families: Incurvariidae, Adelidae, Tineidae, Gracillariidae, Choreutidae, Glyphipterigidae, Yponomeutidae, Plutellidae, Oecophoridae, Tortricidae, Crambidae, Pyralidae and Pterophoridae

Since Victorian times, moths have traditionally been divided into two broad classes: macro-moths (or just moths) that are generally large; and micro-moths that are generally small. In Britain and Ireland there are upwards of 900 different macro-moths and around 1,600 micro-moths. The division is, however, somewhat arbitrary because some micros are bigger than some macros. Most micro-moths are regarded as being more primitive than macro-moths, as many have incomplete mouthparts and do not feed – but even this is not a watertight distinction since a few of the macros also cannot feed.

Many micro-moths regularly fly during the day but because they are so small and often fly quickly, they can be hard to see and identify. Even with a good photograph, it may be impossible to separate similar-looking species. For this reason, only a few species have been included in this book. These have been selected to give an example of the tremendous diversity of families in this complex group and to illustrate their key features.

The Green Longhorn is a tiny green-tinged moth that is one of about a dozen Longhorns in the family Adelidae. It dances round the upper branches of oak trees or Hazel on sunny days in early summer, and although its forewing length is only about 6 mm, males have antennae that are over three times as long as their wing length. The diverse Tortrix family (Tortricidae) has about 400 members in Britain and Ireland. Although they are small, many are very colourful and attractive and they occur in a wide range of habitats. The Crambidae is also a diverse family but the identification of many species is usually relatively easy, particularly if you have taken a photograph for reference. One of the commonest and most distinctive species is the Small Magpie, which ventures into gardens from May to September. Also in the Crambidae family is the *Crambus* genus of grass-moths, which are more challenging to identify.

If you see a brown or white moth standing on long legs with its wings held out sideways at right-angles to its body, it will be a member of the Plume family (Pterophoridae). Many of this family are grassland species and are seen commonly, often hanging onto a grass stem or flying slowly low down in the grass.

Of course, a few moths can be a nuisance. Given the chance, the Common Clothes-moth, will lay its eggs in woollen clothes and, when the caterpillars hatch, they eat the garment leaving tell-tale holes. Another problem species, which only arrived in Britain in 2002, is the Horse-chestnut Leaf-miner. Its tiny caterpillars feed within the leaves of Horse-chestnut trees, causing them to go rusty-brown in late summer. Although the trees recover, their green appearance is spoilt, and they may eventually be weakened.

But the vast majority of micro-moths do no harm at all and have an essential purpose in the natural world. Moths and their eggs, caterpillars and pupae provide a continuous source of food for birds, bats and other members of the animal kingdom. Some of our favourite garden birds rely upon moth caterpillars to feed their young and eat vast quantities of them. And moths that visit flowers (particularly macro-moths) are important for the pollination of many crops and plants.

Names

As there are so many micro-moths they have not all been given widely accepted English names. Most are known just by their formal scientific name. English names are, however, used in this book and follow those adopted by the National Biodiversity Network, which lists all the species known to occur in the British Isles **www.nbn.org.uk**.

Limacodidae – micro macro-moths

Two moths that are classified as macros rather than micros, even though they do not have developed mouthparts, are the **Festoon** *Apoda limacodes* and the **Triangle** *Heterogenea asella*. They are curious, rather nondescript little moths which, when settled, have the shape of a conical tent. They usually fly at night but, very occasionally, might be seen flying in sunshine high up in oak or beech woodland. They belong to a very large worldwide family of mainly tropical moths, the Limacodidae, some of whose caterpillars are spectacular, with stinging spines.

Festoon *Apoda limacodes* FL: 11 mm (× 4)

Triangle *Heterogenea asella* FL: 6 mm (× 4)

Adelidae: male Green (Oak) Longhorns (FL: 6 mm)

Some examples showing the variability of micro-moths

Tortricidae: **Green Oak Tortrix**
(FL: 11 mm)

Tortricidae: male **Arched Marble**
(FL: 7 mm)

Gracillariidae: **Horse-chestnut Leaf-miner**
(FL: 4 mm)

Pyralidae: **Rosy-striped Knot-horn**
(FL: 12 mm)

Pterophoridae: **White Plume**
(FL: 14 mm)

Tineidae: **Common Clothes-moth**
(FL: 6 mm)

Crambidae: **Small Magpie**
(FL: 15 mm)

Crambidae: **Hook-streak Grass-veneer**
(FL: 10 mm)

×10 **Feathered Bright** *Incurvaria masculella* **130**

The Feathered Bright is a deep brown colour, sometimes tinged with purple, with two white triangular patches on the lower edge of its forewings. When the moth is resting, its wings form a tent-like shape with these patches lying along the ridge of the tent, where they are easy to see. This is an unusual micro-moth because the antennae of males are strongly feathered. Most micro-moths have thread-like antennae, which females of this species have too.

Its caterpillars behave in an unusual way. At first they bore into leaves, usually preferring Hawthorn, and eat the inner spongy tissue. However, as they grow bigger, they leave their leaf and crawl down to the ground. Once there, they usually continue feeding on dead leaves on the ground where they then pupate. Curiously, they will have brought a portion of their original leaf down to the ground with them and curl this up to form a casing within which they form their pupa.

Feathered Brights are common throughout much of Britain except north-west Scotland and parts of Ireland. They fly in sunshine early in the season and are frequently seen in woodland where Hawthorn shrubs are in flower in late April and May, sometimes straying into gardens and parks.

Common, found throughout most of Britain and much of Ireland	
Where found:	Woodland and scrubby areas where Hawthorn grows, also parks and gardens
When flying:	Late April–May
Forewing length:	6–8 mm
Larval foodplants:	Hawthorn and other deciduous trees

Similar species: This is one of five similar-looking members of the Incurvariidae family of micro-moths

179

× 10

Green (Oak) Longhorn

Adela reaumurella **150**

There are over a dozen different members of the longhorn family in Britain and Ireland, all of which have long, thin antennae. The antenna length of a male Green Longhorn is about 3 times its forewing length. The females' antennae are about half the length of those of the male, but are still remarkably long. They have metallic dark-green forewings and lighter hindwings. At rest, they have a characteristic tent-like shape, which is the same as for all longhorns. Longhorns fly in sunshine, sometimes in swarms around treetops or around the protruding branches of taller bushes.

Their caterpillars have the strange habit of forming a portable protective case round themselves, using leaf fragments stitched together with silken thread. They develop on the ground, within their portable case. This is found amongst dead leaves, usually under oak, but also birches and probably other trees. As the caterpillars grow, feeding on dead vegetable matter, they extend their case by adding leaf fragments. Pupation occurs inside their case under leaf-litter on the ground.

Common in England and Wales; local in parts of Scotland (although absent from northern Scotland) and in Ireland

Where found:	Found in many habitats, including woodland, scrub, heathland, fens and marshy ground
When flying:	Mid-April–June
Forewing length:	7–9 mm
Larval foodplants:	Not known, but finishes life as a caterpillar on the ground feeding on dead leaves

Similar species: Two members of the Longhorn family are similar, Early Longhorn *Adela cuprella* and Meadow Longhorn *Cauchas* (*Adela*) *rufimitrella* but both are (slightly) smaller, with shorter antennae and more of a bronzy colour

Discarded pupal and leaf case

×10 # Common Clothes-moth

Tineola bisselliella 236

The Common Clothes-moth is one of several species of clothes-moth that are often seen in our homes. However, identification can be difficult and microscopic examination may be necessary to confirm identification. The Case-bearing Clothes-moth *Tinea pellionella* is also common and looks similar except that it has a greyer tinge.

These troublesome little moths lay their eggs in clothes, with most damage being done to woollen garments. When their eggs hatch, caterpillars feed on the fibrous material, leaving the tell-tale holes that are so easily recognized. Often, several tiny caterpillars may be found together, sheltering in a silky cover they have woven for themselves. In a bad infestation, this silky material may become a dense, woven mat with many caterpillars living together. It is probable that the move away from untreated woollen products has reduced the damage caused by caterpillars of clothes-moths, with the drier atmosphere of centrally heated houses also being a contributory factor.

Clothes-moths live indoors all their lives and will continue breeding throughout the year if conditions are warm enough.

Common, although less so in Scotland and Ireland	
Where found:	Warm houses
When flying:	Year-round
Forewing length:	5–7 mm
Larval foodplants:	Woollen and other animal materials

Similar species: There are many similar species in the family Tineidae

× 10

Horse-chestnut Leaf-miner

Cameraria ohridella **366a**

The tiny Horse-chestnut Leaf-miner is a recent arrival in Britain. It was first recorded on Wimbledon Common in 2002 but has now spread to most of England and Wales. It will probably soon be found across the whole of Britain and Ireland. An infected Horse-chestnut tree provides a home for thousands of moths and, when disturbed, they may be seen swarming around its branches.

The leaves turn prematurely brown, and look patchy where the caterpillars are mining the heart of the leaf. The caterpillars pupate inside their leaf. At present, there is no practicable control measure. Trees are not thought to be permanently damaged and recover the next spring until the cycle repeats itself. It is possible, though, that repeated infestation may weaken trees and make them more susceptible to disease.

Common, spreading across most of Britain and probably into Ireland	
Where found:	Hedges, parks and gardens with Horse-chestnut trees
When flying:	May–October; there are two or more overlapping broods
Forewing length:	3·5–5 mm
Larval foodplants:	Leaves of Horse-chestnut and, occasionally, Sycamore trees

There are several leaf miner moths that look similar, but they do not feed on Horse-chestnut trees.

Look for the characteristic leaf damage caused by the tiny caterpillars burrowing below the top skin of the leaves and eating the soft material underneath.

×10 **Common Nettle-tap**   *Anthophila fabriciana* **385**

The Common Nettle-tap is indeed common, occurring throughout a large part of the world, from China right across Asia and Europe. In Britain and Ireland, it may be found anywhere that nettles grow, whether in woodland, along hedgerows or in gardens. It is a very small, dark-brown moth, speckled with pale markings and with two white bars on the outer edge of each forewing. It has a long flight season, from late spring until the end of autumn and there are at least two broods. Swarms of adult moths can sometimes be found buzzing around clumps of nettles.

Common Nettle-tap caterpillars feed on Common Nettle and occasionally on Pellitory-of-the-wall (a non-stinging member of the nettle family that often grows in cracks on old walls). They are light fawn in colour, spotted with dark brown, and live in a web on the surface of leaves that they curl upwards.

Common	
Where found:	Open woodland, hedgerows, gardens
When flying:	May–October
Forewing length:	5–7 mm
Larval foodplants:	Common Nettle (Stinging Nettle), Pellitory-of-the-wall
Similar species: None	

× 10 **Speckled Fanner**

Glyphipterix thrasonella **397**

There are seven species in the genus *Glyphipterix* in Britain and Ireland. They all look similar but vary in size from a forewing length of 3–4 mm for the smallest species up to 5–8 mm for the largest, which is the Speckled Fanner. When settled, the indented shape of their wing edges has the effect of making them look as if they have a tail that sweeps upwards. They all have the curious habit of slowly raising and lowering their wings when resting, rather than keeping still.

The Speckled Fanner has brassy-coloured wings with shining whitish cross-streaks. However, these markings may be much reduced, and the brass appear tarnished.

Look for it (and its similar-looking relations) flying around rushes on wet grassland and moorland. They are often abundant where they are found and will fly continuously in summer sunshine.

The Speckled Fanner's life history is not fully known. Its caterpillars are believed to burrow into the stems (or seeds) of rushes and to keep out of sight there until they emerge as adults.

Common where rushes grow	
Where found:	Wet moorland, bogs, grassland
When flying:	May–August
Forewing length:	5–8 mm
Larval foodplants:	Rushes

Similar species: Other members of the same genus

×6 **Spindle Ermine** *Yponomeuta cagnagella* 427

This is a common member of the 'small ermine' group of micro-moths (genus *Yponomeuta*). Together with the Thistle Ermine (a micro-moth in the Pyralidae family) and the Ermine group of macro-moths, they derive their name from the ermine robes worn by nobility. Historically, these were sewn from the winter coat of stoats and were white with small black spots. Most of the ermine moths are white or buff and speckled with dark spots, with the 'small ermine' species being white or greyish with black spots.

There are eight species in the 'small ermine' group. Many are superficially very similar, and a few are extremely difficult to identify by their wing pattern. The presence of their larval foodplant is the best indicator of the species.

Spindle Ermines feed on the leaves of spindle bushes and trees. They are on the wing in mid-summer and occasionally can be found in large numbers. Their caterpillars, which are yellowish-green with black spots, live together. Like most other 'small ermine' species, they feed gregariously in wispy silken webs, which can be extensive. Although Spindle Ermines are not regular day-flyers, they can often be found by day resting on their larval webs. There are two other 'small ermine' species that feed on spindles, but their webs are never as extensive as the major infestations caused by the Spindle Ermine.

Common in much of England, Wales and Ireland. More local in north-east and northern Scotland, but seemingly absent from much of western Scotland	
Where found:	Scrub, hedgerows, wherever foodplants grow
When flying:	June–September
Forewing length:	10–13 mm
Larval foodplants:	Leaves of spindle bushes and trees in both their deciduous and evergreen forms

Similar species: Other moths in the 'small ermine' group; a distinguishing feature of the Spindle Ermine is the pure white edging to its forewings

× 10 **Diamond-back Moth**

Plutella xylostella 464

The Diamond-back Moth is a member of the family Plutellidae, all of which have the same upswept tail as the Speckled Fanner (*page 184*). They often rest with their front higher than their rear and their antennae pointing forwards. In comparison, the Speckled Fanner holds its antennae pointing backwards.

If you grow cabbages, you will almost certainly have seen this micro-moth, or evidence of its caterpillars. It has whitish markings along the ridge of its resting wings and sometimes looks as if its front legs are longer than its back legs. Its greenish-yellow caterpillars eat the underside of cabbage leaves but they do not chew right through and the transparent-looking upper epidermis is left intact. As a consequence, the leaves end up with white patches.

Although Diamond-back Moths may be found at any time of year, including during the winter, they are most abundant during the summer months. Numbers fluctuate from year to year and it is a migratory species with large numbers sometimes appearing overnight near the coast.

Can be common throughout much of Britain and Ireland	
Where found:	**Wherever cabbages are grown**
When flying:	Continuously brooded, but commonest in the summer
Forewing length:	6–9mm
Larval foodplants:	Members of the cabbage family

Similar species: Other members of the family Plutellidae

×10 **White-shouldered House-moth**   *Endrosis sarcitrella*   **648**

Although house-moths are not strictly day-flying, they are frequently encountered by day. There are two members of the family Oecophoridae that live in houses and outbuildings: the White-shouldered House-moth and its rather drabber-looking relation the Brown House-moth *Hofmannophila pseudospretella*. Both are slightly bigger than the Common Clothes-moth (*page 181*). During the day, they rest on inside walls with their wings spread flatter than a clothes-moth, before coming to life in the evening. White-shouldered House-moth has a noticeable white head and shoulders, which the Brown House-moth lacks, and they have an altogether brighter appearance. They are also slightly smaller than the Brown House-moth.

Their grub-like caterpillars feed on a wide range of dead animal and vegetable material, which they search out anywhere in the house, behind skirting and between floorboards. As their diet includes dry cereals and natural fibres, they can sometimes become a nuisance.

Common throughout much of Britain and Ireland	
Where found:	Indoors in houses, buildings and sheds (as well as outdoors)
When flying:	Continuously brooded, found throughout the year
Forewing length:	6–9 mm
Larval foodplants:	Dead vegetable and animal material

Similar species: Brown House-moth *Hoffmanophila pseudospretella* (which lacks the white head and shoulders and several rarer members of the same family).

Brown House-moth
Hoffmanophila pseudospretella
(FL: 8–13 mm)

×6 **Green Oak Tortrix** *Tortrix viridana* `1033`

The Tortrix family (Tortricidae) is large and diverse, but there is no mistaking this little green moth. It can often be found resting on oak leaves on sunny days in May and June. It is easily disturbed and then flutters among the branches before settling again. There is only one similar species, which is the much rarer Cream-bordered Green Pea *Earias clorana*. However, that species is a nocturnal macro-moth in the family Noctuidae which, as its name suggests, has a cream border to the wings; it also has a different foodplant, feeding on sallows and willow, rather than oak. The Green Oak Tortrix may be found wherever oak trees grow and in some years may be abundant.

The caterpillars, which are pale greyish-green with tiny black spots, feed from within a leaf that they have rolled around themselves for protection. In a year when they are abundant, caterpillars have been known to strip a fully grown tree of its leaves. As well as oak, other deciduous trees are sometimes used, including Beech, Hornbeam, and Sweet Chestnut.

Common in England and Wales; less widely recorded in Scotland and Ireland	
Where found:	Woodland, scrub and hedgerows with oak trees
When flying:	May–June/July, occasionally into August
Forewing length:	9–12 mm
Larval foodplants:	Leaves of oak trees and, sometimes, Beech, Hornbeam and other deciduous trees

Similar species: Cream-bordered Green Pea *Earias clorana*, but this is a Nationally Scarce macro-moth that feeds on willows and is not regarded as a day-flyer

×6 **Arched Marble**   *Olethreutes arcuella*   1080

Like the Green Oak Tortrix, the Arched Marble is a member of the Tortrix family. However, it looks completely different and is easily recognized by its blue-grey streaks and tiny yellow patches on an orangey-brown ground-colour. Throughout the summer, it may be found resting in sunshine on a leaf or flying round deciduous trees. Look in open woodland glades and rides, areas of recent coppice, and on wooded areas of heathland. Its dark-brown caterpillars feed on withered and dead leaves on the ground.

The Tortrix family has several similar-looking species that fly during the day, usually in afternoon sunshine, but this one is colourful and easy to identify. It is, however, fairly scarce. Although it can be found throughout the British Isles, it is local everywhere and very local in Scotland and Ireland.

Fairly rare; found locally in Britain and Ireland	
Where found:	Open woodland glades and rides, wooded heathland
When flying:	May–August
Forewing length:	5–9 mm
Larval foodplants:	Decaying leaves

Similar species: Reasonably distinctive, but there are many similar-sized *Tortrix* moths

An introduction to the grass-moths

The family Crambidae is a large and diverse group of micro-moths, of which eight are covered in this book (*pages 191–198*). It includes the grass-moths, which is a collective term used for a group of closely related species that are very similar in appearance.

They rest with their wings held tightly in a tent-like position and with their antennae swept back over the body. There are many different grass-moths, several of which are widespread and common and they can occasionally be found in large numbers. As their name suggests, they are usually found in grassy situations. A typical example of a grass-moth, the Hook-streak Grass-veneer *Crambus lathoniellus*, is shown opposite and four other species that are common and widely distributed, and regularly encountered during the day, are illustrated below.

Satin Grass-veneer
Crambus perlella (FL: 11–14 mm)

Inlaid Grass-veneer
Crambus pascuella (FL: 11–13 mm)

Straw Grass-veneer
Agriphila straminella (FL: 8–10 mm)

Garden Grass-veneer
Chrysoteuchia culmella (FL: 9–12 mm)

The Satin Grass-veneer *Crambus perlella* may be unmarked, shining whitish, or suffused with lighter greyish streaks. The Inlaid Grass-veneer *C. pascuella* has a long white streak on the forewing (as do some related species), whereas the Straw Grass-veneer *Agriphila straminella* is pale-straw coloured, sometimes with an obscure streak. The Garden Grass-veneer *Chrysoteuchia culmella* can be distinguished by the combination of a metallic forewing fringe and an elbowed cross-line near the edge of its forewing. Although Satin Grass-veneer and Inlaid Grass-veneer are often found in damper grasslands, they are not restricted to these habitats. The Garden Grass-veneer and Straw Grass-veneer are perhaps more frequent in drier grasslands. All fly in the summer months, with the Inlaid Grass-veneer often the earliest to appear, being found from May onwards.

×6 # Hook-streak Grass-veneer *Crambus lathoniellus* 1301

The Hook-streak Grass-veneer is a common moth that may be found almost anywhere in Britain and Ireland on open grassland. Adult moths are easily disturbed by walking through grass and sometimes are very abundant. They frequently fly short distances before settling, with their wings closely folded, on grass stems or lower down amongst grass tufts where they can be harder to see. They rest with their wings held tightly in the characteristic grass-moth position and with their antennae swept back over their body. Females are generally paler than the males. Unless disturbed, they mostly fly late in the afternoon as well as at night, when they are attracted to light.

The caterpillars of this species bore low down into the stems of a wide range of different grasses.

There are many other species of grass-moth that are common and are easily disturbed by day (four of which are shown opposite). Their caterpillars feed on grasses or sedges, and the adult moths look rather similar.

Typical habitat of grass-moths like the Hook-streak Grass-veneer

Common; found throughout Britain and Ireland	
Where found:	Open grassland anywhere
When flying:	May–August
Forewing length:	9–11 mm
Larval foodplants:	Many different grasses

Similar species: This is one of several similar grass-moths that fly by day, particularly in the afternoon or early evening, or are easily disturbed

×6 # Small Purple and Gold (Mint Moth) *Pyrausta aurata* 1361

This pretty micro-moth has two English names: on the National Biodiversity Network's website it is called the Small Purple and Gold, but to gardeners it is often known as the Mint Moth because it is sometimes seen fluttering around garden mint. Its pinkish-coloured caterpillars feed on garden mint and other members of the labiate family. As they mature, they spin leaves together and form a silken web for protection.

The main distinguishing feature between the adults of this species and the Common Purple and Gold is the colour of the pale markings on their otherwise dark hindwings. The Small Purple and Gold has golden hindwing markings, whereas the Common Purple and Gold has pale yellow or whitish markings. A possible source of confusion is the Small Yellow Underwing (*page 154*), a macro-moth in the family Noctuidae that is about the same size as both these species. However, the Small Yellow Underwing does not have a purple tinge to its forewings.

Common in England, eastern Wales and southern Scotland; rare elsewhere	
Where found:	Grassland, especially chalk downland, gardens, quarries, open woodland, marshy ground
When flying:	March–September in two broods
Forewing length:	7–9 mm
Larval foodplants:	Mints, Calamint, Marjoram and other members of the labiate family

Similar species: Common Purple and Gold and some other rarer members of the same genus; also the Small Yellow Underwing (*page 162*)

The gold markings on the hindwings distinguish the Small Purple and Gold from the slightly larger Common Purple and Gold

×6 **Common Purple and Gold** *Pyrausta purpuralis* 1362

This species tends to be slightly larger than the Small Purple and Gold, but otherwise the two are very similar. Caterpillars of this species usually feed on thymes or Corn Mint and, like the Small Purple and Gold, have the habit of drawing their foodplant's leaves together by silken threads and living inside them for protection. There are two broods each year, but the second brood is often more abundant than the first. Adult moths may be seen from late March to early September on chalk downland as they flutter low above the grassland vegetation.

The Common Purple and Gold has pale yellow to whitish hindwing markings that help to distinguish it from the golden hindwing markings of the Small Purple and Gold. Also, there are (usually) three joined golden patches making a golden stripe on their forewings, whereas the Small Purple and Gold's forewings have only one main golden patch.

Common in England and Wales; more local in Ireland and south-west Scotland	
Where found:	Dry calcareous grassland; also coastal grassland and, occasionally, gardens
When flying:	Late March–early September in two broods
Forewing length:	7–11 mm
Larval foodplants:	Thymes and Corn Mint

Similar species: Small Purple and Gold and other members of the same genus, particularly Scarce Purple and Gold *Pyrausta ostrinalis* (this has a thinner and more continuous golden stripe on its forewings); also the Small Yellow Underwing (*page 154*)

The markings on the hindwings are pale yellow to whitish

×6 # Wavy-barred Sable   *Pyrausta nigrata* 1366

Eight species of *Pyrausta* have been recorded in Britain and Ireland, all of which fly in sunshine or on warm, overcast days. Three of these have a black or brown background-colour, rather than purple or red as in the Small and Common Purple and Golds (*pages 192–193*), and sometimes settle with their hindwings showing. All three are grassland species and are the same size, but the most eye-catching is the Wavy-barred Sable.

Wavy-barred Sables are found on calcareous grassland in the south of England and in north Wales, and have been reported on limestone pavement in the Lake District. In sunshine, they move rapidly from flower to flower, keeping low over the ground, so you have to act quickly to take a photograph. Their close relatives the Straw-barred Pearl *P. despicata* and Silver-barred Sable *P. cingulata* have wider distributions: the former is also found on heathland and coastal sites and is therefore more common and widespread; the latter is scarcer. The three species can usually be identified by the pattern of their wing markings.

Local, mainly in the south of England and north Wales	
Where found:	Dry calcareous grassland
When flying:	Mid-April–October in two broods
Forewing length:	7–8 mm
Larval foodplants:	Thyme, Wild Marjoram, Corn Mint, Woodruff and probably other wild herbs

Similar species: There are two similar micro-moths in the *Pyrausta* genus, *Pyrausta cingulata* (with a single, straighter stripe and no white spot) and *Pyrausta despicata* (browner, with less distinct wavy stripes)

Silver-barred Sable
Pyrausta cingulata (FL: 7–8 mm)

Straw-barred Pearl
Pyrausta despicata (FL: 7–9 mm)

×4 # Lesser Pearl

Sitochroa verticalis **1371**

The Lesser Pearl is an attractive straw-yellow colour and is distinguished by the heavily marked and pronounced grid-like pattern on the underside of its wings. It is one of two members of its genus, the other being the Sulphur Pearl *Sitochroa palealis*, which is about the same size but very pale, almost whitish in colour. Both are locally distributed in southern England and south Wales and can be easily disturbed from their grassy habitats.

Caterpillars of both species feed in a silken web on the flowers and developing seeds of various herbaceous plants. They are greyish-green with black markings. Lesser Pearl caterpillars feed on a number of species including Creeping Thistle, goosefoots and Perennial Wall-rocket. Sulphur Pearl caterpillars choose Wild Carrot and Moon Carrot.

Within the wider family Crambidae, there are several other moths that can be confused with the Lesser Pearl, including the Bordered Pearl *Paratalanta pandalis* and Translucent Pearl *P. hyalinalis*, which can both be found by day. All the pearl moths are distributed in the southern half of England, but the Bordered Pearl has also been found farther north in Lancashire and Scotland, as well as in Ireland.

Local, mainly in East Anglia and parts of southern England	
Where found:	Rough pasture, waste ground, field margins
When flying:	May–September, with a partial second brood
Forewing length:	12–15 mm
Larval foodplants:	Perennial Wall-rocket, goosefoots, Creeping Thistle and probably other herbaceous plants

Similar species: There are other similar micro-moths (mentioned in the text).

Lesser Pearl (*left*) and the very slighter larger but much paler **Sulphur Pearl** *Sitochroa palealis* (*right*)

×4 # Brown China-mark *Elophila nymphaeata* `1345`

The Crambidae family includes several 'china-mark' species. They are named after the pattern on their wings which looks rather like the identification marks that Chinese porcelain manufacturers put on their products. They are all curious moths whose habitat is ponds and slow-flowing river margins.

Their pale, pinkish-brown caterpillars feed on waterplants, initially mining a leaf, but later living in a floating case made from leaf fragments. The floating case is attached to the underside of a leaf where the larva feeds, making small holes in the leaf surface. Before pupating, the larva forms a cocoon attached to a plant stem just below the water level.

Adult moths fly on summer evenings and are readily disturbed from waterside vegetation during the day, sometimes in numbers. Two of the four 'china-mark' species that are resident in Britain and Ireland are quite local, but two are more widely found and the Brown China-mark is the most widespread.

Common; found throughout Britain and Ireland although scarcer and more localized in Scotland	
Where found:	Edges of ponds and slow-moving rivers and canals
When flying:	June–September
Forewing length:	12–16mm
Larval foodplants:	Water plants and pondweeds

Similar species: There are three other resident 'china-marks' that look somewhat similar

Mother of Pearl

×4

Pleuroptya ruralis **1405**

This is one of the largest 'micro-moths' and is larger than many moths that are classed as macro-moths. It flies in a wide range of habitats, including woodland, downland, waste ground and gardens throughout much of Britain and Ireland. It is usually possible to get a good view of a settled Mother of Pearl because it stretches out its wings when at rest so that the hindwings are uncovered. Reflection of light in sunshine gives a moth the pearly appearance that justifies its name.

Common Nettles provide the usual foodplant, from which adult moths are easily disturbed by day. Their greyish-green caterpillars make a home for themselves by folding over a leaf and living inside it. They hibernate through the winter, but first descend to the warmer micro-climate at ground level where they spin themselves a cocoon in which they stay until the spring. As the temperature rises, they resume feeding, before pupating inside a rolled leaf in about June.

Common, except in the north of Scotland and parts of Ireland	
Where found:	Waste ground, scrub, woodlands, hedgerows, downland and gardens
When flying:	June–October, sometimes later
Forewing length:	15–17 mm
Larval foodplants:	Common Nettles, but also leaves of elm trees are used

Similar species: There are similarities with some other micro-moths in the Crambidae family, but these are all smaller

× 4

Small Magpie

Anania (= Eurrhypara) hortulata `1376`

There are two magpie moths in Britain and Ireland. One is a macro-moth called simply the Magpie *Abraxas grossulariata*; the other is this species, the Small Magpie, which is classed as a micro-moth. Although not a habitual day-flyer, the Small Magpie is seen much more often because it is frequently disturbed from rest in patches of Common Nettles.

The Small Magpie is common and widespread in central and southern England and in Wales, and common, although more local, in Scotland and Ireland. It has a wide choice of habitats, including gardens and waste ground. There is only one brood and its rather colourless caterpillars keep out of sight as they feed from a rolled-up leaf in late summer. They spend the winter sheltering in a silken cocoon, only pupating the following spring. Their main foodplant is Common Nettle, but woundworts and other herbaceous plants are used, including mints and bindweeds.

Common, except in north-east Scotland and central Ireland	
Where found:	Waste ground, scrub, hedgerows and gardens
When flying:	May–September, sometimes earlier or later
Forewing length:	13–16 mm
Larval foodplants:	Nettles, woundworts, mints, bindweeds

Similar species: The Magpie *Abraxas grossulariata* is larger.

The larger **Magpie** *Abraxas grossulariata* (FL: 18–25 mm) is only occasionally seen flying during the daytime (except in Scotland), and is not usually classed as a day-flying moth.

×4 Rosy-striped Knot-horn

Oncocera semirubella 1441

This is an eye-catching little moth that is easily disturbed from short grass on chalk downland during sunny weather, usually flying close to the ground. It has pink-and-yellow forewings, normally with a whitish stripe along their leading edge. The name 'knot-horn' is derived from the knots of scales standing up like tiny horns that a male moth has at the base of its antennae. When resting, the moth's long antennae are laid back over the wings.

There are several species of knot-horn, most of which are associated with a single specific foodplant, such as a pine, oak, heather or Gorse, and most do not fly readily by day. The Rosy-striped Knot-horn is the exception, and by far the most attractive. It is found on open calcareous grassland and vegetated shingle where its preferred foodplant is Common Bird's-foot-trefoil, although it also feeds on other low herbaceous plants, such as White Clover. Its greenish-grey caterpillars feed in dense silken webs during the spring. Although a local species, primarily of southern England, it is quite common on the North Downs.

Local, primarily in southern and eastern England, but recorded from Northumberland and southern Ireland	
Where found:	Chalk downland, coastal margins, limestone cliffs, vegetated shingle
When flying:	June–August, sometimes later
Forewing length:	11–14 mm
Larval foodplants:	Common Bird's foot-trefoil, and possibly Horseshoe Vetch, clovers and other downland species
Similar species: None	

199

×4 # Brown Plume

Stenoptilia pterodactyla **1509**

Plume moths look completely different from all other moths and rather like a small daddy-long-legs (crane-fly). They stand up on long legs, have a long, slender body and hold their narrow wings out sideways. But plume moths have four wings (a forewing and hindwing on each side), not just one wing each side like a crane-fly, and their wings are of completely different construction. Usually, their forewings have two thin spars with closely spaced bristles sticking out sideways; the hindwings have three spars with bristles. As each spar and bristles looks like a feather, the wings as a whole resemble a plume of feathers.

Brown Plume moths fly in one generation during mid-summer, in open woodland and along hedgerows and verges, grassland and, sometimes, gardens. They are easily disturbed from rest during the day. When resting, adult moths hold their wings at right-angles to their body with their forewings largely covering their hindwings, forming a T–shape. Their caterpillars feed on Germander Speedwell, chewing their way into the stems to hibernate during the winter. The following spring they emerge to feed on the flowers and are well camouflaged, being pale greenish-yellow in colour.

Common; more local in the north and in Ireland	
Where found:	Woodland rides, hedgerows, grassy verges
When flying:	June and July, sometimes slightly earlier or later
Forewing length:	10–13 mm
Larval foodplant:	Germander Speedwell

Similar species: There are many other brownish-coloured plume moths; this is one of the commonest and the most widely distributed

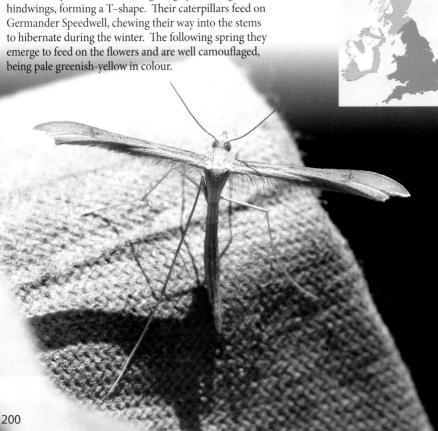

×4 # White Plume

Pterophorus pentadactyla **1513**

This pure white plume moth looks strangely out of place on a grassy bank. Readily disturbed by day, they are easy to see and flutter about quite slowly, making their identification quite straightforward. There are several other whitish plume moths, but these are off-white in colour, smaller and less likely to be seen.

Like the Brown Plume, its forewings consist of two 'feathery' spars and its hindwings three spars, hence its specific name *pentadactyla* which means 'five-fingered'. When settled, the hindwings are hidden by its forewings. Then, only two feathery spars show, sticking out like two plumed fingers. They are divided at their outer tip. The caterpillars overwinter and when mature are pale green with yellow markings and white hairs. They feed on most species of bindweed and adult moths can be found readily in the vicinity of bindweeds in summer.

Common, although more local in the north and in Ireland	
Where found:	Grassy rides, banks and verges, hedgerows, waste ground
When flying:	April to August, sometimes earlier
Forewing length:	12–16 mm
Larval foodplants:	Leaves and flowers of bindweeds

Similar species: Several other light-coloured plume moths but they are all smaller and none has the brilliant white of this species

White Plume moth in usual resting pose and with wings extended (*inset*)

Page	Bradley & Fletcher No.	Preferred habitat (see pages 16–19)		1 Gardens and parkland 2 Meadows and farmland 3 Downland 4 Heathland and moorland	5 Woodland 6 Coastal dunes and cliffs 7 Wetland and fenland 8 Uplands							
		SPECIES	Scientific name	1	2	3	4	5	6	7	8	
FORESTERS												
30	163	Forester	*Adscita statices*		●	●	●	●	●	●		
31	164	Cistus Forester	*Adscita geryon*			●						
32	165	Scarce Forester	*Jordanita globulariae*			●						
BURNETS												
35	166	Scotch Burnet	*Zygaena exulans*								●	
39	167	Slender Scotch Burnet	*Zygaena loti*						●			
34	168	New Forest Burnet	*Zygaena viciae*						●			
38	169	Six-spot Burnet	*Zygaena filipendulae*	●	●	●	●	●	●	●		
36	170	Five-spot Burnet	*Zygaena trifolii*			●						
37	171	Narrow-bordered Five-spot Burnet	*Zygaena lonicerae*		●	●	●	●	●			
33	172	Transparent Burnet	*Zygaena purpuralis*						●			
CLEARWINGS												
42	370	Hornet Moth	*Sesia apiformis*	●	●			●				
43	371	Lunar Hornet Moth	*Sesia bembeciformis*				●	●		●		
45	372	Dusky Clearwing	*Paranthrene tabaniformis*					●				
46	373	Currant Clearwing	*Synanthedon tipuliformis*	●	●							
44	369a	Raspberry Clearwing	*Pennisetia hylaeiformis*	●	●							
48	374	Yellow-legged Clearwing	*Synanthedon vespiformis*	●	●			●				
49	375	White-barred Clearwing	*Synanthedon spheciformis*				●	●				
51	376	Welsh Clearwing	*Synanthedon scoliaeformis*				●	●				
47	377	Sallow Clearwing	*Synanthedon flaviventris*				●	●				
50	378	Orange-tailed Clearwing	*Synanthedon andrenaeformis*			●		●				
52	379	Red-belted Clearwing	*Synanthedon myopaeformis*	●	●			●				
53	380	Red-tipped Clearwing	*Synanthedon formicaeformis*							●		
54	381	Large Red-belted Clearwing	*Synanthedon culiciformis*				●	●				
55	382	Six-belted Clearwing	*Bembecia ichneumoniformis*			●		●				
56	383	Thrift Clearwing	*Synansphecia muscaeformis*					●				
57	384	Fiery Clearwing	*Pyropteron chrysidiformis*					●				
EGGARS, EMPEROR, KENTISH GLORY												
60	1637	Oak Eggar	*Lasiocampa quercus*			●	●	●	●	●		
61	1638	Fox Moth	*Macrothylacia rubi*				●	●	●	●		
62	1643	Emperor Moth	*Saturnia pavonia*		●		●	●	●	●		
63	1644	Kentish Glory	*Endromis versicolora*				●	●				
HOOK-TIPS												
64	1646	Oak Hook-tip	*Watsonalla binaria*	●	●			●				
65	1647	Barred Hook-tip	*Watsonalla cultraria*					●				

The species in this table are listed in taxonomic (Bradley & Fletcher) order

Flight season

■ = whole country; ■ = north; ■ = south;
■ = generation overlap; ■ = occasional

Main larval foodplant

(the usual caterpillar foodplant is given, but for some species there are many alternative foodplants)

Conservation status (CS), BAP and legislative protection

(see pages 210–213)

J F M A M J J A S O N D	Main larval foodplant	CS	BAP	Legislation
	Sorrels		UK	NERC (S41 & S42)
	Rock-rose	B		
	Knapweeds	A		
	Crowberry etc.	R	Sc	
	Common Bird's-foot-trefoil	R	UK	
	Meadow Vetchling etc.	EN	UK	W&C (S5)
	Bird's-foot-trefoils			
	Bird's-foot-trefoils			
	Meadow Vetchling etc.		Sc	
	Wild Thyme	A	Sc	
	Poplars	B		
	Willows			
	Aspen etc.	EX?		
	Currants	B		
	Raspberry			
	Oaks	B		
	Alder and birches	B		
	Downy Birch	R	Sc	NERC (S42)
	Sallows	B		
	Wayfaring-tree etc.	B		
	Apple etc.	B		
	Willows	B		
	Birches, Alder	B		
	Bird's-foot-trefoils, vetches	B		
	Thrift	B		
	Docks, sorrels	EN	UK	W&C (S5), NERC (S41)
	Heathers, Bilberry etc.			
	Heathers, Bilberry etc.			
	Heathers, birches etc.			
	Birches, Alder	R	Sc	
	Oaks		UK	
	Beech			

Key to CS (Conservation status) column:

EX	Extinct in Britain	EN	Endangered	VU	Vulnerable
R	Nationally Rare	A	Nationally Scarce A	B	Nationally Scarce B

Key to BAP (Biodiversity Action Plan) column:

UK UK BAP Priority Sp. (UK = research)
Sc On Scottish Biodiversity List
NI Priority Species in Northern Ireland

Page	Bradley & Fletcher No.	SPECIES	Scientific name	1	2	3	4	5	6	7	8
GEOMETRIDS											
68	1661	Orange Underwing	*Archiearis parthenias*				●	●			
69	1662	Light Orange Underwing	*Archiearis notha*					●			
70	1665	Grass Emerald	*Pseudoterpna pruinata*				●		●		
71	1682	Blood-vein	*Timandra comae*	●	●			●		●	
72	1687	Lace Border	*Scopula ornata*			●					
73	1698	Purple-bordered Gold	*Idaea muricata*				●			●	
74	1704	Silky Wave	*Idaea dilutaria*			●					
75	1721	Balsham Carpet	*Xanthorhoe biriviata*		●					●	
76	1723	Red Carpet	*Xanthorhoe decoloraria*						●		●
77	1724	Red twin-spot Carpet	*Xanthorhoe spadicearia*	●	●	●	●	●	●	●	
78	1727	Silver-ground Carpet	*Xanthorhoe montanata*	●	●	●	●	●	●	●	
79	1728	Garden Carpet	*Xanthorhoe fluctuata*	●	●	●	●	●	●		
86	1731	Chalk Carpet	*Scotopteryx bipunctaria*		●				●		
93	1732	Shaded Broad-bar	*Scotopteryx chenopodiata*	●	●	●	●	●	●		
94	1733	Lead Belle	*Scotopteryx mucronata*				●				
95	1734	July Belle	*Scotopteryx luridata*				●	●	●	●	
84	1737	Small Argent and Sable	*Epirrhoe tristata*				●				●
81	1738	Common Carpet	*Epirrhoe alternata*	●	●	●	●	●	●	●	
80	1740	Galium Carpet	*Epirrhoe galiata*			●	●		●		
92	1742	Yellow Shell	*Camptogramma bilineata*	●	●	●	●	●	●	●	
88	1743	Yellow-ringed Carpet	*Entephria flavicinctata*			●			●		
89	1744	Grey Mountain Carpet	*Entephria caesiata*								●
82	1753	Striped Twin-spot Carpet	*Nebula salicata*				●	●	●		●
90	1766	Blue-bordered Carpet	*Plemyria rubiginata*	●	●					●	
91	1776	Green Carpet	*Colostygia pectinaria*	●	●	●	●	●		●	●
99	1780	Slender-striped Rufous	*Coenocalpe lapidata*								●
87	1786	White-banded Carpet	*Spargania luctuata*					●			
85	1787	Argent and Sable	*Rheumaptera hastata*				●	●		●	
96	1805	Heath Rivulet	*Perizoma minorata*			●	●				●
97	1806	Pretty Pinion	*Perizoma blandiata*			●	●				●
98	1807	Grass Rivulet	*Perizoma albulata*			●			●		
83	1809	Twin-spot Carpet	*Perizoma didymata*				●	●	●		
100	1822	Marsh Pug	*Eupithecia pygmaeata*			●		●			
101	1828	Satyr Pug	*Eupithecia satyrata*				●				●
102	1862	Double-striped Pug	*Gymnoscelis rufifasciata*	●	●	●	●	●			
103	1866	Manchester Treble-bar	*Carsia sororiata*				●				
104	1867	Treble-bar	*Aplocera plagiata*	●	●	●	●	●	●		
105	1868	Lesser Treble-bar	*Aplocera efformata*	●	●	●			●	●	
106	1870	Chimney Sweeper	*Odezia atrata*		●	●	●				
107	1875	Small White Wave	*Asthena albulata*					●			
108	1878	Drab Looper	*Minoa murinata*					●			
109	1894	Latticed Heath	*Chiasmia clathrata*	●	●	●	●	●			

Flight season
■ = whole country; ■ = north; ■ = south;
■ = generation overlap; ■ = occasional

J F M A M J J A S O N D

Main larval foodplant
(the usual caterpillar foodplant is given, but for some species there are many alternative foodplants)

Conservation status (CS), BAP and legislative protection (see pages 210–213)

Main larval foodplant	CS	BAP	Legislation
Birches	B		
Aspen			
Gorse, Broom etc.			
Docks, sorrels etc.		UK	NERC (S41 & S42)
Thyme, Marjoram etc.	A		
Cinquefoils etc.	B		
Rock-rose	R	UK	NERC (S41 & S42)
Balsam			
Lady's-mantle		UK	NERC (S41 & S42)
Bedstraws etc.			
Cleavers, bedstraws etc.			
Garlic Mustard etc.			
Bird's-foot-trefoils etc.	B	UK	NERC (S41 & S42)
Clovers, vetches		UK	NERC (S41 & S42)
Gorse, Broom etc.			
Gorse, Petty Whin etc.			
Heath Bedstraw			
Bedstraws and Cleavers			
Bedstraws		UK	NERC (S41 & S42)
Bedstraws, Cleavers etc.			
Saxifrages	B	NI	
Heather and Bilberry		UK	NERC (S41 & S42)
Bedstraws			
Blackthorn, Alder etc.			
Bedstraws etc.			
Meadow Buttercup	A		
Willowherbs	A		
Birches, Bog-myrtle	B	UK	NERC (S41 & S42)
Eyebright	B		
Eyebright		NI	
Yellow-rattle			
Bilberry, heathers etc.			
Mouse-ears	B		
Meadowsweet, heathers etc.			
Ivy, Gorse, heathers etc.			
Bilberry, Cowberry etc.	B		
St John's-worts			
St John's-worts			
Pignut			
Hazel, Hornbeam, birches etc.			
Wood Spurge	B	UK	NERC (S41 & S42)
Lucerne, clovers etc.		UK	NERC (S41 & S42)

Page	Bradley & Fletcher No.	SPECIES	Scientific name	1	2	3	4	5	6	7	8
		Preferred habitat (see pages 16–19)		\#1 Gardens and parkland		5 Woodland					

Preferred habitat (see pages 16–19)

1 Gardens and parkland 5 Woodland
2 Meadows and farmland 6 Coastal dunes and cliffs
3 Downland 7 Wetland and fenland
4 Heathland and moorland 8 Uplands

Page	Bradley & Fletcher No.	SPECIES	Scientific name	1	2	3	4	5	6	7	8
110	1895	Netted Mountain Moth	*Macaria carbonaria*								●
111	1896	Rannoch Looper	*Itame brunneata*								●
112	1901	Little Thorn	*Cepphis advenaria*				●				
113	1902	Brown Silver-line	*Petrophora chlorosata*				●	●			
114	1908	Dark Bordered Beauty	*Epione vespertaria*				●				
115	1909	Speckled Yellow	*Pseudopanthera macularia*				●				
116	1928	Belted Beauty	*Lycia zonaria*						●		
117	1929	Rannoch Brindled Beauty	*Lycia lapponaria*				●				
118	1952	Common Heath	*Ematurga atomaria*		●	●	●	●			
119	1954	Bordered White	*Bupalus piniaria*					●			
120	1963	Scotch Annulet	*Gnophos obfuscatus*								●
121	1964	Annulet	*Charissa obscurata*			●	●		●		
122	1965	Black Mountain Moth	*Glacies coracina*								●
123	1966	Black-veined Moth	*Siona lineata*			●					
124	1967	Straw Belle	*Aspitates gilvaria*			●					
125	1968	Yellow Belle	*Semiaspitates ochrearia*						●		
126	1969	Grey Scalloped Bar	*Dyscia fagaria*				●				
127	1970	Grass Wave	*Perconia strigillaria*				●	●			

HAWK-MOTHS

Page	Bradley & Fletcher No.	SPECIES	Scientific name	1	2	3	4	5	6	7	8
132	1982	Narrow-bordered Bee Hawk-moth	*Hemaris tityus*			●	●				
133	1983	Broad-bordered Bee Hawk-moth	*Hemaris fuciformis*			●	●				
131	1984	Hummingbird Hawk-moth	*Macroglossum stellatarum*	●	●	●	●	●	●	●	

TUSSOCKS

Page	Bradley & Fletcher No.	SPECIES	Scientific name	1	2	3	4	5	6	7	8
136	2025	Scarce Vapourer	*Orgyia recens*			●	●		●		
137	2026	Vapourer	*Orgyia antiqua*	●	●		●	●	●	●	
138	2034	Gypsy Moth	*Lymantria dispar*							●	

FOOTMEN, TIGERS, ERMINES

Page	Bradley & Fletcher No.	SPECIES	Scientific name	1	2	3	4	5	6	7	8
139	2036	Dew Moth	*Setina irrorella*			●			●		
140	2039	Red-necked Footman	*Atolmis rubricollis*			●	●				
141	2056	Wood Tiger	*Parasemia plantaginis*			●	●	●			
146	2059	Clouded Buff	*Diacrisia sannio*			●	●	●			
147	2063	Muslin Moth	*Diaphora mendica*	●	●	●		●	●	●	
144	2064	Ruby Tiger	*Phragmatobia fuliginosa*	●	●	●	●	●	●	●	
142	2067	Jersey Tiger	*Euplagia quadripunctaria*	●	●				●		
143	2068	Scarlet Tiger	*Callimorpha dominula*		●				●		
145	2069	Cinnabar	*Tyria jacobaeae*	●	●	●	●	●	●	●	

NOCTUIDS

Page	Bradley & Fletcher No.	SPECIES	Scientific name	1	2	3	4	5	6	7	8
165	2104	Northern Rustic	*Standfussiana lucernea*			●			●		●
150	2118	True Lover's Knot	*Lycophotia porphyrea*				●				●
151	2142	Beautiful Yellow Underwing	*Anarta myrtilli*				●				
152	2143	Small Dark Yellow Underwing	*Anarta cordigera*				●				●
153	2144	Broad-bordered White Underwing	*Anarta melanopa*				●				●
155	2175	Silurian	*Eriopygodes imbecilla*				●				●

Flight season

■ = whole country; ■ = north; ■ = south;
■ = generation overlap; ■ = occasional

Main larval foodplant
(the usual caterpillar foodplant is given, but for some species there are many alternative foodplants)

Conservation status (CS), BAP and legislative protection (see pages 210–213)

J	F	M	A	M	J	J	A	S	O	N	D	Main larval foodplant	CS	BAP	Legislation
												Bearberry	R	UK	
												Bilberry	A		
												Bilberry	B		
												Bracken			
												Aspen etc.	R	UK	NERC (S41)
												Wood Sage, dead-nettles etc.			
												Bird's-foot-trefoils, vetches	R	UK	NERC (S41 & S42)
												Bog-myrtle, Bilberry etc.	A		
												Heathers, clovers			
												Conifers			
												Saxifrages etc.	B		
												Sea Campion, Thrift etc.			
												Crowberry	R		
												Marjoram, knapweeds etc.	EN	UK	**W&C (S5)**, NERC (S41)
												Bird's-foot-trefoils etc.		UK	NERC (S41)
												Wild Carrot, plantains etc.			
												Heathers etc.			
												Heathers etc.			
												Devil's-bit scabious etc.	B	UK	NERC (S41 & S42)
												Honeysuckle	B		
												Lady's Bedstraw etc.			
												Sallows, birches, oaks etc.	VU	UK	NERC (S41)
												Birches, Hazel, elms etc.			
												Broad-leaved trees	EX		
												Lichens	A		
												Lichens			
												Heather, plantains etc.		NI	
												Heathers, plantains etc.			
												Docks etc.			
												Ragworts, plantains etc.			
												Common Nettle, plantains etc.	B		
												Hemp-agrimony etc.			
												Ragworts etc.		UK	NERC (S41 & S42)
												Saxifrages, Harebell etc.			
												Heathers etc.			
												Heathers			
												Bearberry	R	UK	
												Crowberry, Bilberry etc.			
												Bilberry, bedstraws	R		NERC (S42)

Page	Bradley & Fletcher No.	SPECIES	Scientific name	1	2	3	4	5	6	7	8
		Preferred habitat (see pages 16–19)	1 Gardens and parkland · 2 Meadows and farmland · 3 Downland · 4 Heathland and moorland · 5 Woodland · 6 Coastal dunes and cliffs · 7 Wetland and fenland · 8 Uplands								
158	2176	Antler Moth	*Cerapteryx graminis*			●	●				
156	2341	Cloaked Minor	*Mesoligia furuncula*	●		●			●		
157	2344	Least Minor	*Photedes captiuncula*		●	●			●		
159	2352	Dusky Sallow	*Eremobia ochroleuca*		●	●			●		
160	2360	Ear Moth	*Amphipoea oculea*	●	●		●	●	●		
161	2367	Haworth's Minor	*Celaena haworthii*				●			●	
154	2397	Small Yellow Underwing	*Panemeria tenebrata*		●	●			●		
162	2401	Marbled Clover	*Heliothis viriplaca*		●	●		●	●		
163	2402	Shoulder-striped Clover	*Heliothis maritima*				●				
164	2403	Bordered Straw	*Heliothis peltigera*						●		
166	2412	Silver Hook	*Deltote uncula*				●			●	●
167	2413	Silver Barred	*Deltote bankiana*				●			●	
168	2441	Silver Y	*Autographa gamma*	●	●	●	●	●	●		
170	2444	Gold Spangle	*Autographa bractea*		●	●	●	●			
169	2447	Scarce Silver Y	*Syngrapha interrogationis*				●				
173	2462	Mother Shipton	*Callistege mi*		●	●	●		●		
172	2463	Burnet Companion	*Euclidia glyphica*		●	●		●			
171	2465	Four-spotted	*Tyta luctuosa*		●	●					
174	2466	Blackneck	*Lygephila pastinum*		●	●		●		●	
175	2470	Small Purple-barred	*Phytometra viridaria*			●	●	●	●		
MICRO-MOTHS											
179	130	Feathered Bright	*Incurvaria masculella*	●				●			
180	150	Green (Oak) Longhorn	*Adela reaumurella*				●	●		●	
181	236	Common Clothes-moth	*Tineola bisselliella*								
182	366a	Horse-Chestnut Leaf-miner	*Cameraria ohridella*	●				●			
183	385	Common Nettle-tap	*Anthophila fabriciana*	●	●			●			
184	397	Speckled Fanner	*Glyphipterix thrasonella*				●			●	
185	427	Spindle Ermine	*Yponomeuta cagnagella*	●	●			●			
186	464	Diamond-back Moth	*Plutella xylostella*	●	●	●	●	●	●	●	
187	648	White-shouldered House-moth	*Endrosis sarcitrella*	●	●	●	●	●		●	
188	1033	Green Oak Tortrix	*Tortrix viridana*		●			●			
189	1080	Arched Marble	*Olethreutes arcuella*					●			
191	1301	Hook-streak Grass-veneer	*Crambus lathoniellus*		●	●	●				
196	1345	Brown China-mark	*Elophila nymphaeata*				●			●	
192	1361	Small Purple and Gold (Mint Moth)	*Pyrausta aurata*	●	●	●	●			●	
193	1362	Common Purple and Gold	*Pyrausta purpuralis*	●	●	●			●		
194	1366	Wavy-barred Sable	*Pyrausta nigrata*			●					
195	1371	Lesser Pearl	*Sitochroa verticalis*	●	●				●		
198	1376	Small Magpie	*Anania (Eurrhypara) hortulata*	●	●				●		
197	1405	Mother of Pearl	*Pleuroptya ruralis*	●	●	●		●			
199	1441	Rosy-striped Knot-horn	*Oncocera semirubella*		●				●		
200	1509	Brown Plume	*Stenoptilia pterodactyla*		●			●			
201	1513	White Plume	*Pterophorus pentadactyla*	●	●						

J	F	M	A	M	J	J	A	S	O	N	D	Main larval foodplant	CS	BAP	Legislation
												Grasses			
												Grasses			
												Sedges	R		
												Grasses			
												Grasses		UK	NERC (S41 & S42)
												Common Cotton-grass etc?		UK	NERC (S41 & S42)
												Mouse-ears			
												Restharrow, campions etc.	R		
												Coss-leaved Heath etc.	R	UK	NERC (S41)
												Restharrow, mayweeds etc.			
												Grasses, sedges			
												Grasses	VU		
												Bedstraws, clovers etc.			
												Common Nettle, Ground-ivy etc.			
												Heather, Bilberry etc.			
												Clovers, grasses etc.			
												Clovers, Lucerne etc.			
												Field Bindweed	VU	UK	NERC (S41)
												Tufted Vetch			
												Milkworts			
												Hawthorn etc.			
												Dead leaves			
												Wool etc.			
												Horse-chestnut			
												Common Nettle			
												Rushes			
												Spindle			
												Cabbages			
												Detritus			
												Oaks etc.			
												Dead leaves			
												Grasses			
												Pond weeds			
												Mints			
												Thymes			
												Thymes etc.			
												Wall-rocket etc.			
												Common Nettle etc.			
												Common Nettle etc.			
												Bird's-foot-trefoils etc.			
												Germander Speedwell			
												Bindweed			

Isle of Portland

Conservation and legislation

Many of the day-flying moths covered in this book are the subject of nature conservation concern. This section summarizes the current position regarding their conservation status in the UK, the UK Biodiversity Action Planning framework, and the domestic legislation that applies.

Red Data Books

The International Union for Conservation of Nature (IUCN) Red List of Threatened Species, also known as The IUCN Red List or Red Data Book, is a comprehensive and regularly updated inventory of the global conservation status of species of plants and animals. Species are classified according to extinction risk based on established criteria. These criteria include the rate of decline, population size, area of geographic distribution, and degree of population and distribution fragmentation.

The purpose of the Red Lists is to communicate conservation issues to the public and policy-makers. Species are categorized as either **Extinct** (EX); **Extinct in the Wild** (EW); **Critically Endangered** (CR); **Endangered** (EN); **Vulnerable** (VU); **Near Threatened** (NT); **Least Concern** (LC); **Data Deficient** (DD); or **Not Evaluated** (NE). The term 'threatened' is used for species categorized as either **Critically Endangered**, **Endangered** or **Vulnerable**.

The Red List criteria can also be used to assess the threat status of species at a regional level. Although moths have not yet been classified using IUCN criteria in the UK, a similar approach has broadly been followed in preparing the British

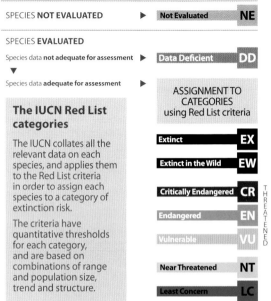

The IUCN species category assignment process

SPECIES **NOT EVALUATED** ▶ Not Evaluated **NE**

SPECIES **EVALUATED**

Species data **not adequate for assessment** ▶ Data Deficient **DD**
▼
Species data **adequate for assessment** ▶ ASSIGNMENT TO CATEGORIES using Red List criteria

The IUCN Red List categories

The IUCN collates all the relevant data on each species, and applies them to the Red List criteria in order to assign each species to a category of extinction risk.

The criteria have quantitative thresholds for each category, and are based on combinations of range and population size, trend and structure.

Extinct **EX**
Extinct in the Wild **EW**
Critically Endangered **CR**
Endangered **EN**
Vulnerable **VU**
Near Threatened **NT**
Least Concern **LC**

THREATENED

Red Data Book, whereby species were categorized based on the degree of threat. In the case of day-flying moths, these are included in ***British Red Data Books 2: Insects*, edited by D. B. Shirt, Joint Nature Conservation Committee, 1987**. The latest categorizations are summarized in a spreadsheet that can be downloaded from the Joint Nature Conservation Committee's website at **www.jncc.defra. gov.uk/page-3408.**

One species, the Gypsy Moth, is categorized as **Extinct** in Britain and the species account is annotated as follows:

British Red Data Book (Extinct)

Four species are categorized as **Endangered**: Black-veined Moth, Fiery Clearwing, New Forest Burnet and Transparent Burnet. These are indicated in the species accounts as follows:

British Red Data Book (Endangered)

A further three species are categorized as **Vulnerable**: Four-spotted, Scarce Vapourer, and Silver Barred. These are indicated in the species accounts as follows:

British Red Data Book (Vulnerable)

Nationally Rare species

Species are also assessed against criteria such as their presence in 10 km x 10 km squares (hectads) of the Ordnance Survey (OS) National Grid. Species or subspecies with small populations that are not currently considered to meet the thresholds for categorization as Endangered or Vulnerable, but are at risk, are included in the British Red List as 'Rare' if they occur in 15 or fewer hectads, and are termed 'Nationally Rare'. Sixteen day-flying moth species meet this criterion:

Balsam Carpet
Belted Beauty
Black Mountain Moth
Dark Bordered Beauty
Kentish Glory
Least Minor
Marbled Clover
Netted Mountain Moth
Scarce Forester
Scotch (Mountain) Burnet
Shoulder-striped Clover
Silky Wave
Silurian
Slender Scotch Burnet
Small Dark Yellow Underwing
Welsh Clearwing

These species are annotated as follows:

Nationally Rare

Nationally Scarce species

Species that are found in between 16 and 100 hectads are conventionally defined as 'Nationally Scarce' (also termed Nationally Notable). This category is subdivided into 'Nationally Scarce A' for species that occur in 16 to 30 hectads, and 'Nationally Scarce B' if found in between 31 and 100 hectads.

Nationally Scarce A species

Eight species of day-flying moths are listed as Nationally Scarce A:

Dew Moth
Lace Border
Rannoch Brindled Beauty
Rannoch Looper
Scarce Forester
Slender-striped Rufous
Transparent Burnet
White-banded Carpet

These species are annotated as follows:

Nationally Scarce A

Nationally Scarce B species

A total of 26 day-flying moths are listed as Nationally Scarce B:

Argent and Sable
Broad-bordered Bee Hawk-moth
Chalk Carpet
Cistus Forester
Currant Clearwing
Drab Looper
Heath Rivulet
Hornet Moth
Jersey Tiger
Large Red-belted Clearwing
Light Orange Underwing
Little Thorn
Manchester Treble-bar
Marsh Pug
Narrow-bordered Bee Hawk-moth
Orange-tailed Clearwing
Purple-bordered Gold
Red-belted Clearwing
Red-tipped Clearwing
Sallow Clearwing
Scotch Annulet
Six-belted Clearwing
Thrift Clearwing
White-barred Clearwing
Yellow-legged Clearwing
Yellow-ringed Carpet

These species are indicated in the species accounts as follows:

Nationally Scarce B

Biodiversity Action Plans

Under the UK's Biodiversity Action Plan (UK BAP) **www.jncc.defra.gov.uk/page-5155**, a list of priorities has been drawn up that recognizes the practical issues and actions required for the conservation of habitats and species. This is the Government's response to world concern about nature conservation and fulfils the UK's international obligations under the United Nations.

A Priority Species identified in the UK BAP is generally one that is declining rapidly in the UK. When deciding what to do about conserving these species, many factors have to be considered, such as the chances of achieving a recovery, the cost, the impact on other species, and our national and international obligations.

The UK BAP identifies 28 species of day-flying moth as Priority Species or in need of research (R): Argent and Sable, Belted Beauty, Black-veined Moth, Blood-vein (R), Chalk Carpet, Cinnabar (R), Dark-bordered Beauty, Drab Looper, Ear Moth (R), Fiery Clearwing, Forester, Four-spotted, Galium Carpet (R), Grey Mountain Carpet (R), Haworth's Minor (R), Latticed Heath (R), Narrow-bordered Bee Hawk-moth, Netted Mountain Moth, New Forest Burnet, Oak Hook-tip (R), Red Carpet (R), Scarce Vapourer, Shaded Broad-bar (R), Shoulder-striped Clover, Silky Wave, Slender Scotch Burnet, Small Dark Yellow Underwing and Straw Belle. These are indicated in the species accounts as follows:

UK BAP Priority Species

Butterfly Conservation is Lead Partner for the majority of these species, taking action to conserve them and co-ordinating the efforts of others.

In addition, Local Biodiversity Action Plans have been produced by many local authorities and other bodies. These plans

Argent and Sable (see *page 85*)

aim to deliver conservation at a local level and many day-flying moths are targeted for actions such as surveys, monitoring or more practical conservation measures.

Legislation

The populations of some species of day-flying moth have declined significantly and/or are highly localized. For this reason, they are offered some protection through domestic legislation.

Wildlife and Countryside Act 1981 (as amended)

In the UK, three species of day-flying moth are listed in Schedule 5 of the Wildlife and Countryside Act 1981 (as amended) – Black-veined Moth, Fiery Clearwing and New Forest Burnet. This confers some degree of protection, including prohibiting handling without a licence. The species concerned are annotated in the species accounts as:

LEGALLY PROTECTED: W&C Act (Sched. 5)

The Natural Environment and Rural Communities (NERC) Act

This Act came into force on 1st Oct 2006. Sections 41 (S41) and 42 (S42) of the Act require the Secretary of State to publish a list of habitats and species that are of principal importance for the conservation of biodiversity in England and Wales respectively. The list is used to guide

Fiery Clearwing (see *page 57*)

Black-veined Moth (see *page 123*)

decision-makers such as public bodies, including local and regional authorities, in implementing their duty under Section 40 of the NERC Act 2006, to have regard to the conservation of biodiversity when carrying out their normal functions.

NERC Act S41 (England)

The 24 day-flying moth species covered by this section of the NERC Act are: Argent and Sable, Belted Beauty, Black-veined Moth, Blood-vein, Chalk Carpet, Cinnabar, Dark Bordered Beauty, Drab Looper, Ear Moth, Fiery Clearwing, Forester, Four-spotted, Galium Carpet, Grey Mountain Carpet, Haworth's Minor, Latticed Heath, Narrow-bordered Bee Hawk-moth, Oak Hook-tip, Red Carpet, Scarce Vapourer, Shaded Broad-bar, Shoulder-striped Clover, Silky Wave and Straw Belle. These are coded in the species accounts as:

Legislative listing: NERC Act (S41)

NERC Act S42 (Wales)

The 19 day-flying moth species covered by this section of the NERC Act are: Argent and Sable, Belted Beauty, Blood-vein, Chalk Carpet, Cinnabar, Drab Looper, Ear Moth, Forester, Galium Carpet, Grey Mountain Carpet, Haworth's Minor, Latticed Heath, Narrow-bordered Bee Hawk-moth, Oak Hook-tip, Red Carpet, Shaded Broad-bar, Silky Wave, Silurian and

Welsh Clearwing. These are indicated in the species accounts as:

Legislative listing: NERC Act (S42)

National biodiversity lists

Some species of day-flying moth are included on biodiversity lists that have been drawn up separately in Scotland and Northern Ireland and are underpinned by domestic legislation and/or policy.

The species included on the **Scottish Biodiversity List** are: Argent and Sable, Dark Bordered Beauty, Forester, Kentish Glory, Narrow-bordered Bee Hawk-moth, Narrow-bordered Five-spot Burnet, Netted Mountain Moth, New Forest Burnet, Scotch (Mountain) Burnet, Slender Scotch Burnet, Small Dark Yellow Underwing, Transparent Burnet and Welsh Clearwing. These are indicated in the species accounts as:

Scottish Biodiversity List

The day-flying moths that are listed as Priority Species in **Northern Ireland** are: Argent and Sable, Cinnabar, Ear Moth, Forester, Galium Carpet, Grey Mountain Carpet, Haworth's Minor, Latticed Heath, Narrow-bordered Bee Hawk-moth, Pretty Pinion, Red Carpet, Shaded Broad-bar, Wood Tiger and Yellow-ringed Carpet. These are indicated in the species accounts with the following annotation:

Priority Species (Northern Ireland)

Butterfly and moth conservation

Butterfly Conservation
Saving butterflies, moths and our environment

Founded in 1968, **Butterfly Conservation** is the UK charity dedicated to saving butterflies and moths and their habitats. It runs a wide variety of conservation projects and plays a lead role in protecting the UK's butterfly and moth populations. This work is underpinned by sound scientific research and implemented through detailed Action Plans to reverse population declines. These plans are implemented in collaboration with statutory and voluntary conservation organizations, as well as with corporate partners and individuals. Much of the work is conducted at a landscape scale – more, bigger, better-managed and joined-up sites – to ensure the long-term conservation of threatened species.

In addition, Butterfly Conservation manages over 30 nature reserves and gives advice on over 50 partnership reserves with others. A strong membership supports regional branches throughout the UK. Every year, these branches organize hundreds of field trips, talks and educational courses. Volunteers are involved in monitoring several thousand important localities, and give practical help by joining work parties to manage habitats.

Members are kept up-to-date by the charity's magazine *Butterfly* and a steady stream of reports and papers is available covering detailed scientific news and research. Local branches also produce their own regular newsletters and run their own websites which list events and projects in their area. A wealth of information and links to the Branch websites are available from Butterfly Conservation's website **www.butterfly-conservation.org.**

Recording and monitoring

A central aspect of Butterfly Conservation's work is the gathering of accurate recording and monitoring information on the state of butterflies and moths.

The National Moth Recording Scheme **www.mothscount.org**, which was launched in 2007, is open to all. Everyone interested is encouraged to record their sightings (species, date, number seen, place and grid reference) and send this information to the appropriate County Moth Recorder (whose details are given on the Butterfly Conservation website **www.butterfly-conservation.org**). It is intended to cover the whole of Britain and Ireland by this scheme. It provides important historical data about moth distributions, and how these are changing.

In addition, Butterfly Conservation and the journal Atropos **www.atropos.info** run an annual moth recording event, called Moth Night. Each year there is a theme, and on particular days during the warmest part of the year, recorders are invited to make a special effort to record what they see and

All observers are invited to send details of their findings to the relevant County Moth Recorder. Details are on the Butterfly Conservation site **www.butterfly-conservation.org** – follow the links through:
How you can help >
Recording and monitoring >
National Moth Recording Scheme >
County Moth Recorders

submit their results on the online recording system. There is interest in both day-flying and night-flying species. The full findings each year are published in the journal *Atropos*.

The more-recently started Garden Moth Scheme **www.gardenmoths.org.uk** is primarily devoted to trapping moths at night. Participants run a moth trap once a week throughout the season and submit their results online.

All these schemes are intended to extend to Ireland.

Results for Ireland are given on the Moths of Ireland website, **www.mothsireland.com**, where provisional distribution maps for the principal macro-moths found here are available.

The National Moth Recording Scheme also has provisional distribution maps for macro-moths found in the UK and published in the Butterfly Conservation's *Provisional Atlas of the UK's Larger Moths*. These maps enable recorders to put their own sightings into a wider context and stimulate further recording by identifying coverage gaps at local and national levels.

Further reading

It would not have been possible to complete this book without relying heavily upon previous publications and on information published online on various excellent websites. We are extremely grateful to all their authors and, particularly, to those of the main sources of reference:

***Colour Identification Guide to Moths of the British Isles*, by Bernard Skinner, illustrated by David Wilson, Apollo Books, Denmark, 3rd edition, 2009.**

***Field Guide to the Moths of Great Britain and Ireland*, by Paul Waring and Martin Townsend, illustrated by Richard Lewington, British Wildlife Publishing, Gillingham, 2nd edition, 2009.**

***Field Guide to the Micro-moths of Great Britain and Ireland*, General editor: Phil Sterling, main contributor: Mark Parsons, illustrated by Richard Lewington, British Wildlife Publishing, Gillingham, 2012.**

The first two deal exclusively with macro-moths, the third exclusively with micro-moths.

These excellent books are valuable reference sources, particularly for identifying unusual or difficult moths. Skinner's book shows moths in their traditional display position, as they would appear in a museum tray of set specimens. This is helpful because size is easily judged and the hindwings are exposed. However, Waring and Townsend show many (but not all) moths in their typical resting positions and this can be very helpful in recognizing a species from a photograph. The micro-moth book by Sterling and Parsons is the first compact field guide to this large and diverse group of small moths, and is indispensable as a resource for identifying these tiny creatures. All illustrations are of moths in their resting positions.

Modern books are supplemented by information and, particularly, by photographs published on the web. In the section on *page 217*, a list is provided of the various excellent web resources in this rapidly changing field.

Interest in moths and their collection and preservation began in earnest in Victorian times. The information given may be out-of-date in some cases, but Richard South's books are notable because they were the essential reference for generations of moth enthusiasts and his beautifully written short essays about each species remain a joy to read.

The Moths of the British Isles (2 volumes) by Richard South, Frederick Warne & Co., London, 1932.

and the accompanying

The Caterpillars of British Moths including the eggs, chrysalids and food-plants (2 volumes) by W. J. Stokoe, Frederick Warne & Co., London, 1948.

There are many other good reference books, from which a selection is listed below:

Moths of Great Britain and Ireland by Sean Clancy, Morten Top-Jensen and Michael Fibiger, Bugbook Publishing, Denmark, 2012.
This is a field guide to macro-moths, with good photographs and short descriptions of every species.

British Moths and Butterflies – a photographic guide, by Chris Manley, A&C Black, London, 2008.
This is another collection of excellent photographs of all the macro-moths and some 500 micro-moths, with a sentence or two about each species.

The Butterflies and Moths of Northern Ireland, by Robert Thompson and Brian Nelson, National Museums Northern Ireland, 2006.
This covers all the butterflies and macro-moths recorded in Northern Ireland. A feature of the book is its exceptionally high standard of photography.

Provisional Atlas of the UK's Larger Moths, by Les Hill, Zoë Randle, Richard Fox and Mark Parsons, Butterfly Conservation, Wareham, Dorset, 2010.
A collection of maps of Britain and Northern Ireland showing known distribution records for some 870 macro-moths.

Moths, by E. B. Ford, New Naturalist Series, Collins, London, 1955.
Although old, this is a masterly description of the natural history, structure and physiology of moths which remains very largely equally relevant today. There is now a modern version of this book by the late Mike Majerus, published by Harper Collins in 2002.

The Colour Identification Guide to the Caterpillars of the British Isles: (Macrolepidoptera), by Jim Porter, Apollo Books, Denmark, 2010 (first published in 1997).
A comprehensive, photographic guide that complements Bernard Skinner's book.

Other relevant books include:

Enjoying Moths, by Roy Leverton, 2002 and **The Natural History of Moths, by Mark Young, 1996**, both **published by T. & A. D. Poyser, London.**

In addition, there are many more specialized books. A full bibliography would occupy several pages and the omission above of other titles, including many excellent regional books, and of the vast library of specialized reference books is solely because space is limited and these lists can be obtained elsewhere in the literature.

***A Recorder's Log Book or Label List of British Butterflies and Moths*, J. D. Bradley and D. S. Fletcher, Curwen Books, 1979.**
This was prepared for submitting records to the Biological Records Centre at Monks Wood, as part of one of the first widespread lepidoptera recording schemes in Britain. The Bradley and Fletcher numbers (often shortened to just Bradley Numbers) are shown in the species accounts in this book.

Useful websites

Organizations and journals:

Butterfly Conservation	**www.butterfly-conservation.org**
National Moth Recording Scheme	**www.mothscount.org**
Moths of Ireland	**www.mothsireland.com**
Garden Moths Scheme	**www.gardenmoths.org.uk**
Royal Entomological Society	**www.royensoc.co.uk**
British Entomological & Natural History Soc.	**www.benhs.org.uk**
Amateur Entomologists' Society	**www.amentsoc.org**
Wildlife Trusts	**www.wildlifetrusts.org**
Dublin Naturalists' Field Club	**www.dnfc.net**
Atropos (journal)	**www.atropos.info**
Entomologist's Gazette (journal)	**www.pemberleybooks.com**
British Wildlife (journal)	**www.britishwildlife.com**

Helpful identification websites:

ukmoths	**www.ukmoths.org.uk**
mothshots	**www.mothshots.com**
ukleps	**www.ukleps.org**

These websites are all a great help for identifying moths. The last, particularly, has many good images of eggs, caterpillars and pupae and a link to the UK Lepidopterists Study Group Forum. In addition, many county moth groups have their own website.

Entomological suppliers:

Anglian Lepidopterist Supplies	**www.angleps.com**
Bioquip	**www.bioquip.net**
B&S Entomological Services	**www.entomology.org.uk**
Watkins & Doncaster	**www.watdon.co.uk**

Acknowledgements and photographic credits

The production of this book would not have been possible without the help and cooperation of many people. We are grateful particularly for the support of Butterfly Conservation. Martin Warren, its Chief Executive, was enthusiastically supportive from the beginning, and Mark Parsons, Head of Moth Conservation, devoted a considerable amount of time advising on the text and commenting on the final draft. We are also very grateful to Les Hill of the National Moth Recording Scheme and Angus Tyner of mothsireland.com for providing the data from which our maps have been drawn. Gill Swash provided invaluable assistance as our meticulous proof-reader.

Butterfly Conservation made available its library of images, many of which, with the consent of the original photographers, have been reproduced. But there were still gaps, and many of the photographers acknowledged below searched their files to locate missing images for us. One photograph is often the result of hours of patient fieldwork, and we recognize the contribution of every photographer with gratitude and thanks.

We were offered many more photographs than could be included in this book and thank all who have contributed, including Graham Austin (GA), Paul Brock (PB), Angie Craig (AC), David Green (DG), Brian Hancock (BH), John Kemp (JK), Ian Kimber (IK), Roy Leverton (RL), Andrew Mitchell (AM), Iris Newbery (IN), Mark Parsons (MP), the late Paul Pugh (PP), Keith Tailby (KT) and Martin Warren (MW). Roy Leverton kindly reviewed all the selected images for us and made invaluable comments. We have tried to achieve an accurate colour balance in the reproductions and selected photographs with this in mind. The colouring of individual moths of a particular species can vary considerably, and so we have attempted to show a representative image of each. Every photograph published in the book is credited below, using the photographer's initials above; those taken by the authors are shown using the following initials: Andy and Gill Swash / WorldWildlifeImages.com (AS) and David Newland (DN).

Cover	**Mother Shipton** (AS)	Page 19	Wetland (DN); Upland (DN)
Title page	Burnets in a huddle (PB)	Page 20	**Four-spotted** (DN)
Page 4	**Hummingbird Hawk-moth** (DN)	Page 21	Wisley gardens (DN)
Page 6	**Brimstone** (DN); **Lesser Treble-bar** (DN); **Holly Blue** (DN); **Oak Eggar** (DN); Frenulum (DN)	Page 28	**Six-spot Burnet** (DN)
		Page 29	Larva (DN); Burnets mating (DN); **Forester** (MP); Forester habitat (MP)
Page 7	**Jersey Tiger** (DG); **Vapourer** (DN)	Page 30	**Forester** (DG)
Page 8	**Silver Y** on lavender (DN)	Page 31	**Cistus Forester** (MP)
Page 9	**Six-spot Burnet** (*7 images*) (DN)	Page 32	**Scarce Forester** (DG)
Page 10	Wing scales (DN)	Page 33	**Transparent Burnet** (DG)
Page 13	**Yellow Shell** (DN); **Silver Y** (DN)	Page 34	**New Forest Burnet** (DG)
Page 14	Forester (MP); Burnet (DN); Clearwing (DN); **Oak Eggar** (DN); **Emperor** (IN); **Kentish Glory** (DG); Hook-tip (PB); **Common Carpet** (DN)	Page 35	**Scotch** (**Mountain**) **Burnet** (KT)
		Page 36	**Five-spot Burnet** (DG)
		Page 37	**Narrow-bordered Five-spot Burnet** (PB); (*inset*) (DN)
Page 15	Hawk-moth (PB); **Vapourer** (DN); Footman (DN); **Wood Tiger** (DG); **Muslin** (DG); **Dusky Sallow** (DN); **Small Magpie** (DN); **White Plume** (DN)	Page 38	**Six-spot Burnet** (DG)
		Page 39	**Slender Scotch Burnet** (DG)
		Page 40	Six-belted at lure (DN)
		Page 41	**Six-belted Clearwing** (*top*) (DN); **Raspberry Clearwing** (DN); Raspberry Clearwing habitat (DN); **Six-belted Clearwing** (PB); Cherry Hinton habitat (DN)
Page 16	Garden (DN); Field edge (DN)		
Page 17	Downland (DN); Moorland (DN)		
Page 18	Woodland (DN); Coastal (DN)		

Index

This index includes the English and scientific names, and alternative names, of all the moth species covered in this book. Common names in **bold text** indicate species that are afforded a full account.

Bold red numbers refer to the page on which the main species account can be found. *Italicized blue* numbers indicate the location of other photographs of adult moths or caterpillars. Normal black numbers refer to pages on which species that are not afforded a full account are mentioned.

222